# THE BEAST WITHIN



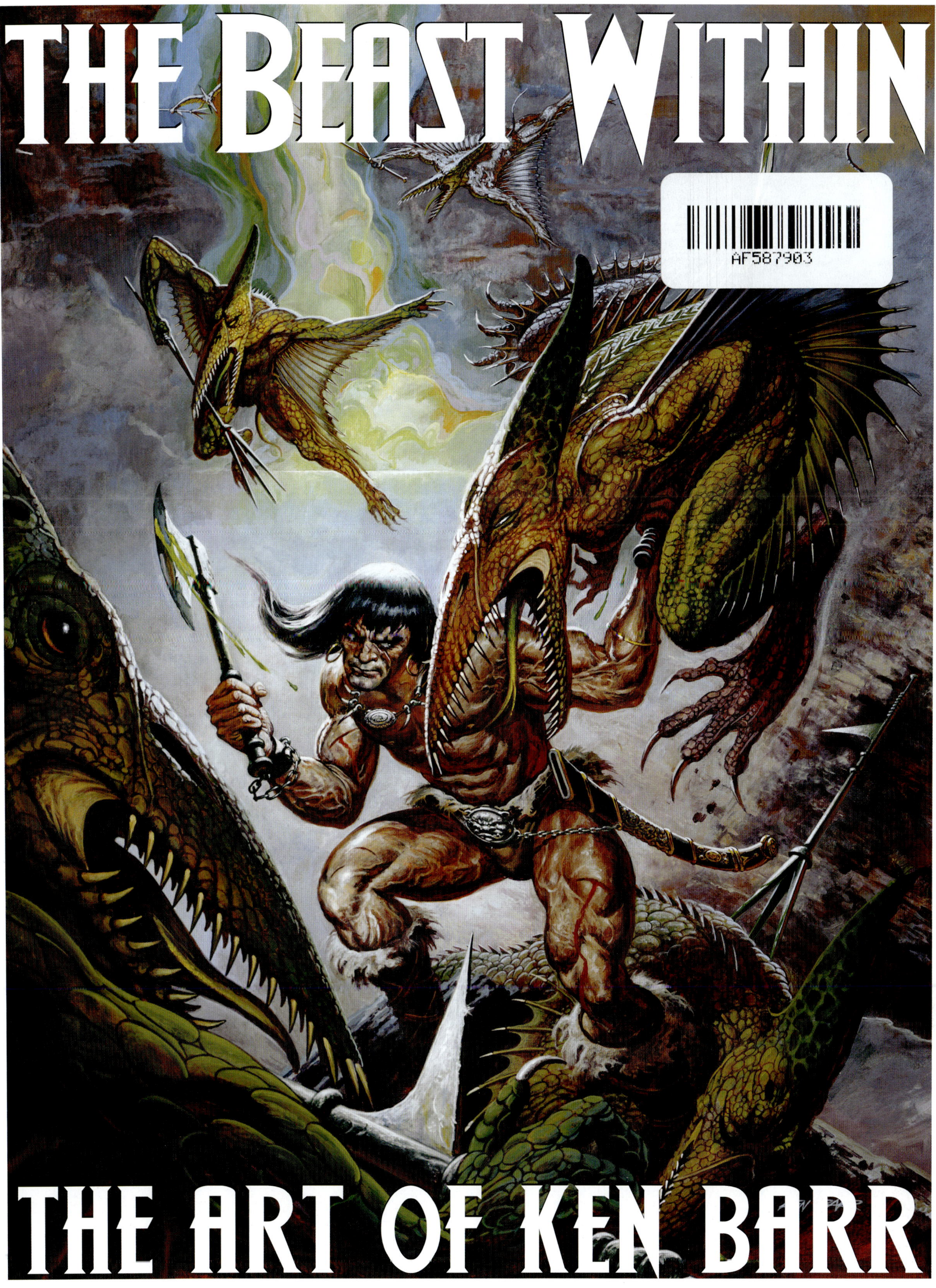

## THE ART OF KEN BARR

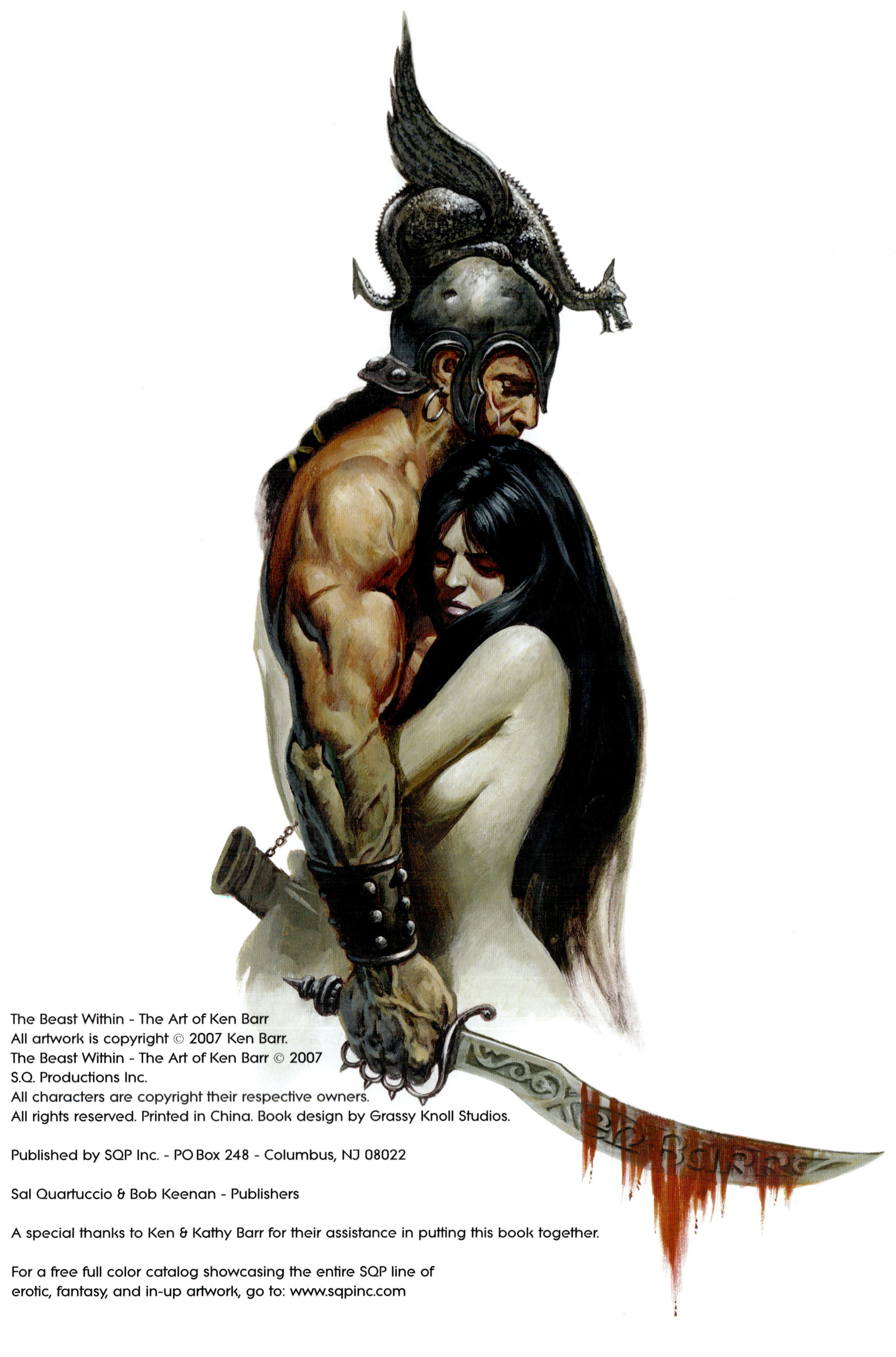

The Beast Within - The Art of Ken Barr

 Printed in China. Book design by Grassy Knoll Studios.

Published by SQP Inc. - PO Box 248 - Columbus, NJ 08022

Sal Quartuccio & Bob Keenan - Publishers

A special thanks to Ken & Kathy Barr for their assistance in putting this book together.

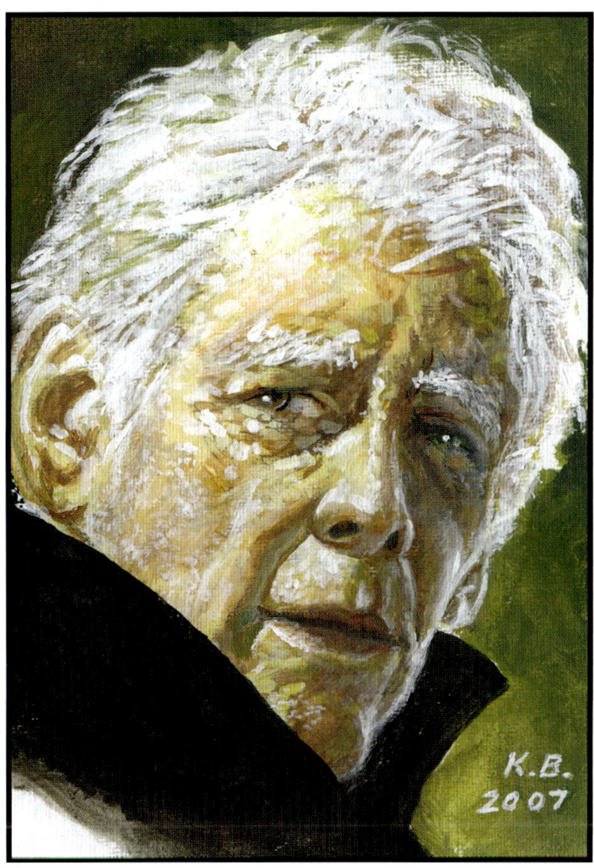


# KEN BARR

A fresh perspective.

That's one of the singular delights that Ken Barr has always brought to his work. Long before the advent of computer-generated art and photo-realistic illustration in comics, Ken brought that fresh perspective to his paintings. It was one thing to see the Hulk bound about in the pages of 2-D comics, but to see this not-so-jolly-green giant realized as a fully rendered 10 foot behemoth as you might see him in the real world? Wow! This was something new in comics, but then Ken has always been an innovator.

Born in Glasgow, Scotland in March of 1933, he was as much a target of Nazi aggression as anyone else on that island by 1940. He, and about fifty other children were evacuated to a crumbling mansion in the remote Scottish Highlands for the duration of the war. Despite the extreme rationing of the time, some pencils and butcher paper gave Ken the ability to escape into worlds of his own making. Even at such a young age, he had an intuitive understanding of perspective, light, shadow, and texture, all of which caught the eye of his teachers. At war's end, Ken returned to Glasgow to finish his schooling and begin an apprenticeship as a lettering artist and commercial designer.

After learning his craft, Ken's career got slightly delayed with a two-year stint in the National Service (where he became the youngest Sergeant in the British Army), which also put him in some exotic locales!

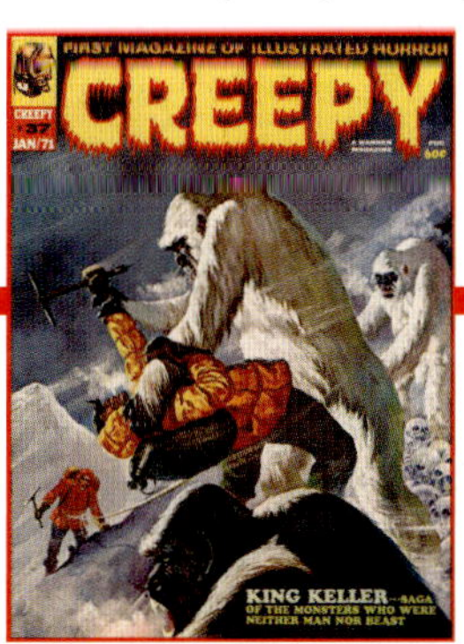


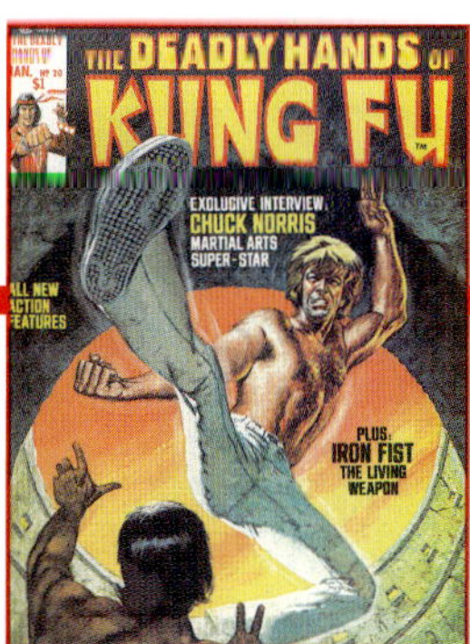


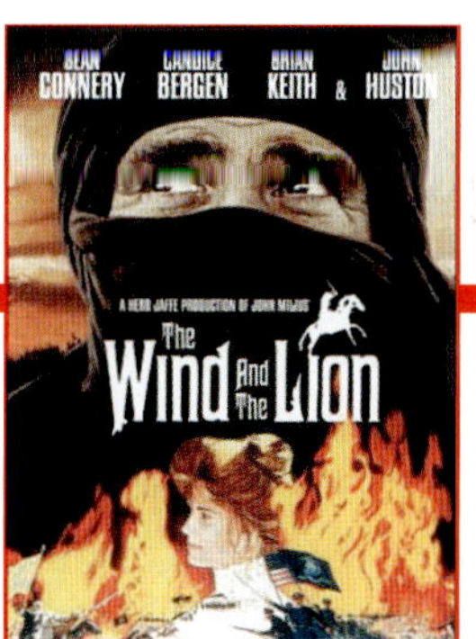


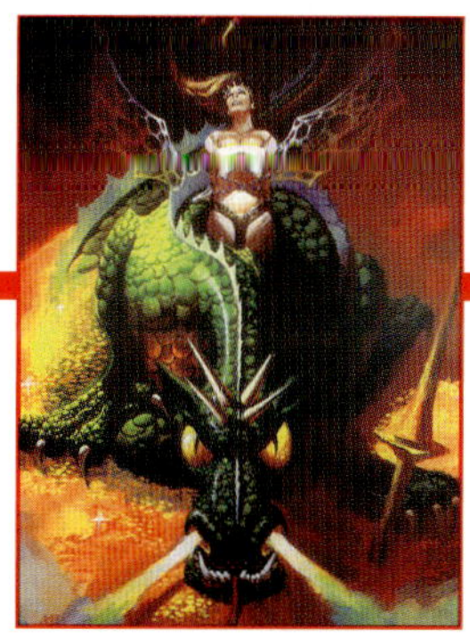

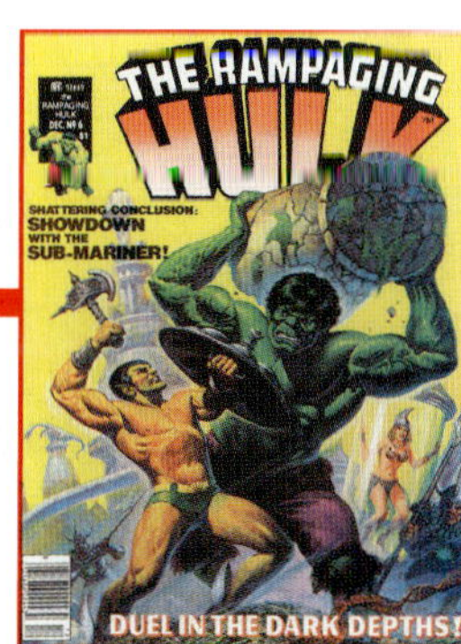


Once back in civilian life, he honed his drawing skills in design studios in Glasgow, Dundee and London. In a neat bit of fortune, Ken was able to dovetail his illustrative talents and recent military career for the **D.C. THOMPSON** company, producing hundreds of painted covers of "**Commando**", a series of WWII adventure books aimed at young boys.

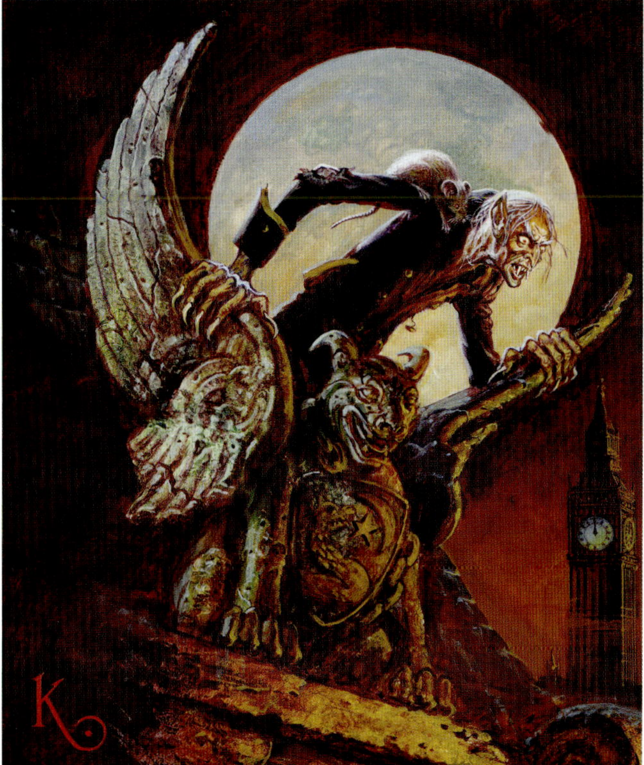

In 1966, on his first visit to the U.S., he met a lovely young American girl by the name of Katharine Griffin. After much trans-Atlantic back and forth, they married a year later. Green card in hand, Ken and his new bride settled in New Jersey, and began thirty-plus years of illustrating the impossible!

Primarily a commercial artist, Ken had standard clients, but it was the work he did on the early **WARREN** magazines like **Eerie** and **Creepy** that gave him a bit of a following. Exploring this weird world of fantasy and horror had him showing up at the 1970 Comic Book Convention in New York City. There he and Kathy would try selling some prints of paintings he had worked up, and to meet some of his fans in person. Here's where it gets personal, because it was at this show that they met a very young and energetic kid from Brooklyn who was extremely interested in Ken's work. The young seventeen year old was Sal Quartuccio, and the project he was working on was a book called "**Phase**", and the iconic cover Ken created is still a classic (featured in all its two-page glory in this book!)

That wraparound cover painting of King Arthur and his men fighting demons is seared into the collective minds of most fantasy art fans! It was ahead of its time, and indicative of what would come next for Ken. His painted covers for **Marvel Comic's** magazine line are among the best the House of Ideas ever produced! Undoubtedly they gave many of today's foremost cover artists a glimpse of what was possible in the medium.

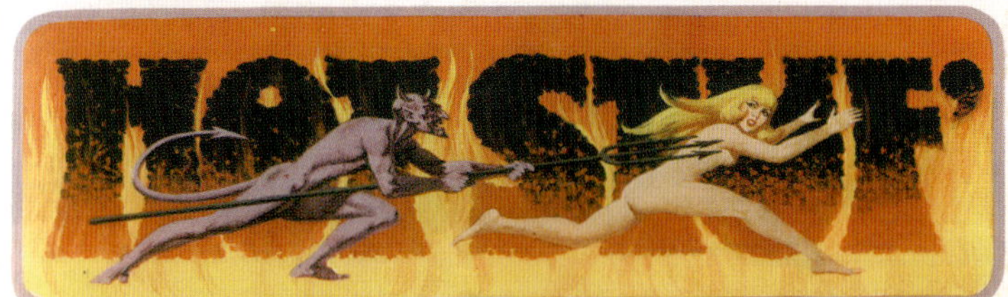


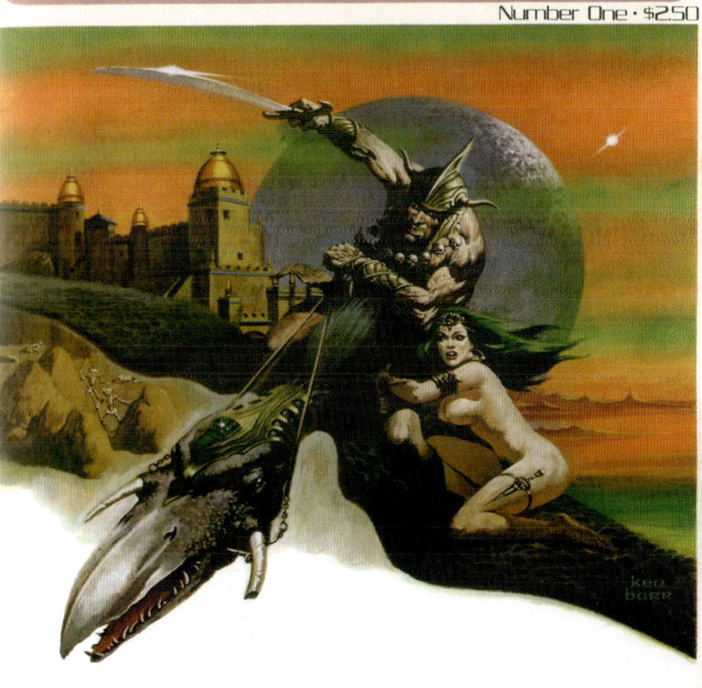


Four years after the Phase book, Ken created the cover art to Sal's next project "**Hot Stuf'**", making that book an immediate best seller.

Ken also knows his way around a pencil and a pen, having illustrated many stories for **DC Comics' Star-Spangled War Stories** and **G.I. Combat**. Again, that two-year stay in the Army paid off with non-stop dividends!

Hollywood has also had the good fortune to have Mr. Barr on board. Ken's work for the movies has included poster art for Clint Eastwood's "**Thunderbolt and Lightfoot**", George Segal's "**The Terminal Man**", and fellow Scots heart-throb Sean Connery's "**Wind and the Lion**", to name just a few assignments.

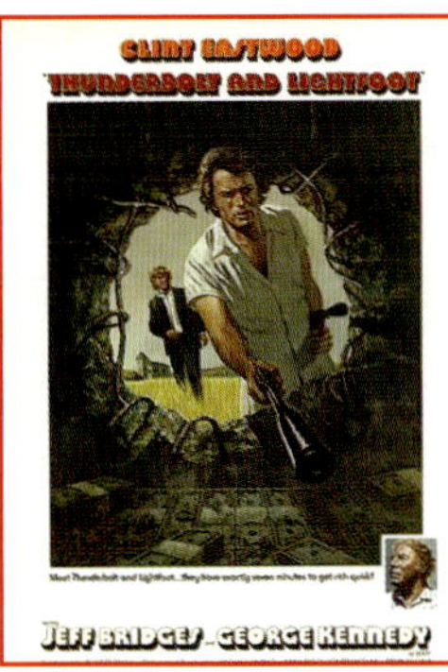


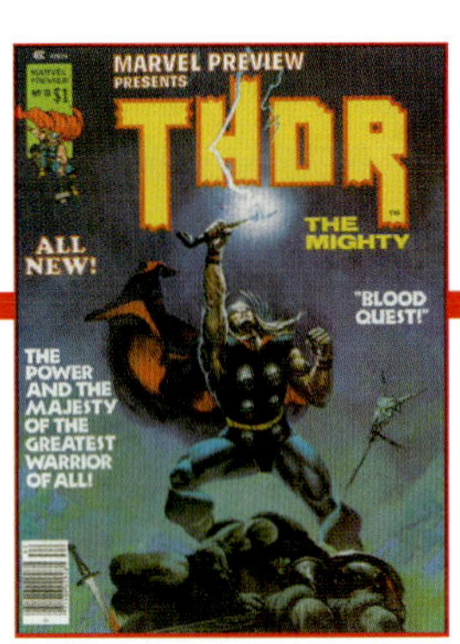


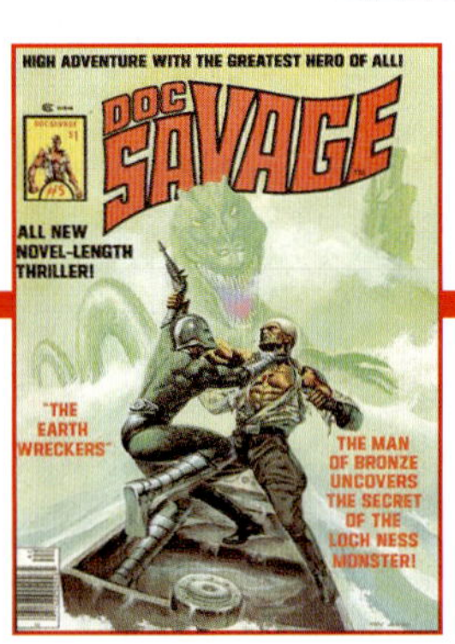


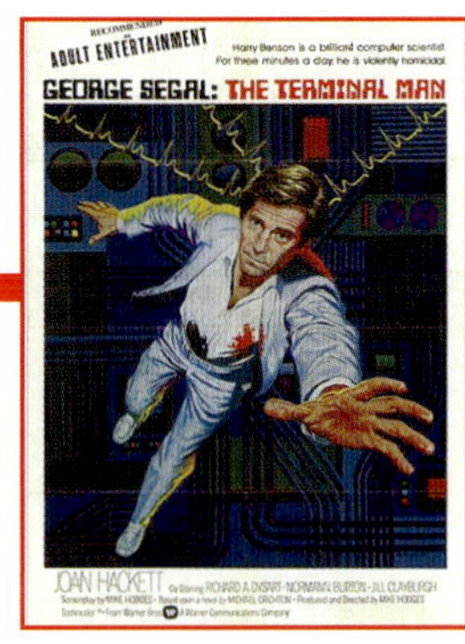


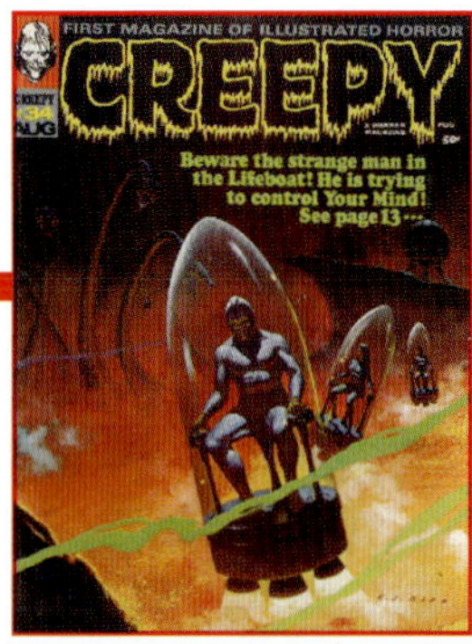


George Lucas, a well-known connoisseur of fantasy art is a bit of a Barr fan as well, and has had Ken do some **Star Wars** related material over the years as well.

Ken has also created a line of unicorn plates for the **Danbury Mint**, and those pieces are among the most highly sought-after items in their entire catalog! In 1994 his prolific collection of paintings was made into a highly-collectible card set "**The Beast Within**" by **Comic Images**.

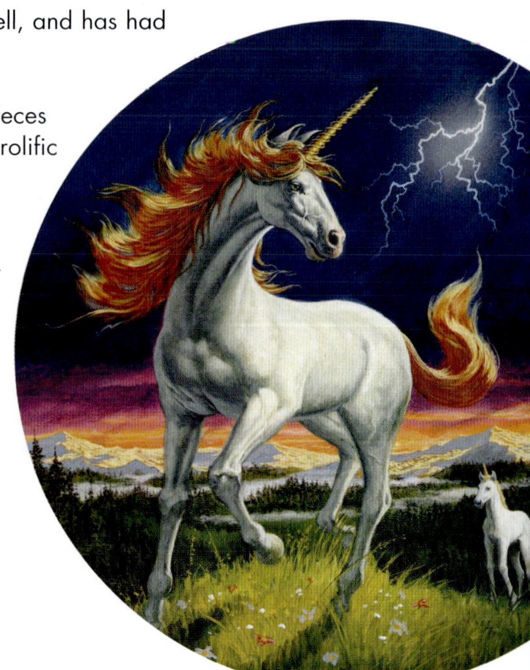

In 1997, Ken retired back to Glasgow, to devote his attention to a long-time labor of love - an illustrated version of Bram Stoker's "**Dracula**", faithful in every way to the original novel. Being an honorary life member of the **Dracula Society of London**, this fully painted book is going to be meticulous in its detail!

Speaking of labors of love, this book is something that's been in the planning stages since that fateful day in New York City, when a truly amazing artist took a chance taking an assignment from an enthusiastic kid, and helped to start a publishing company.

Thanks Ken! This one's for you!

**Sal Quartuccio**
**Bob Keenan**
Publishers

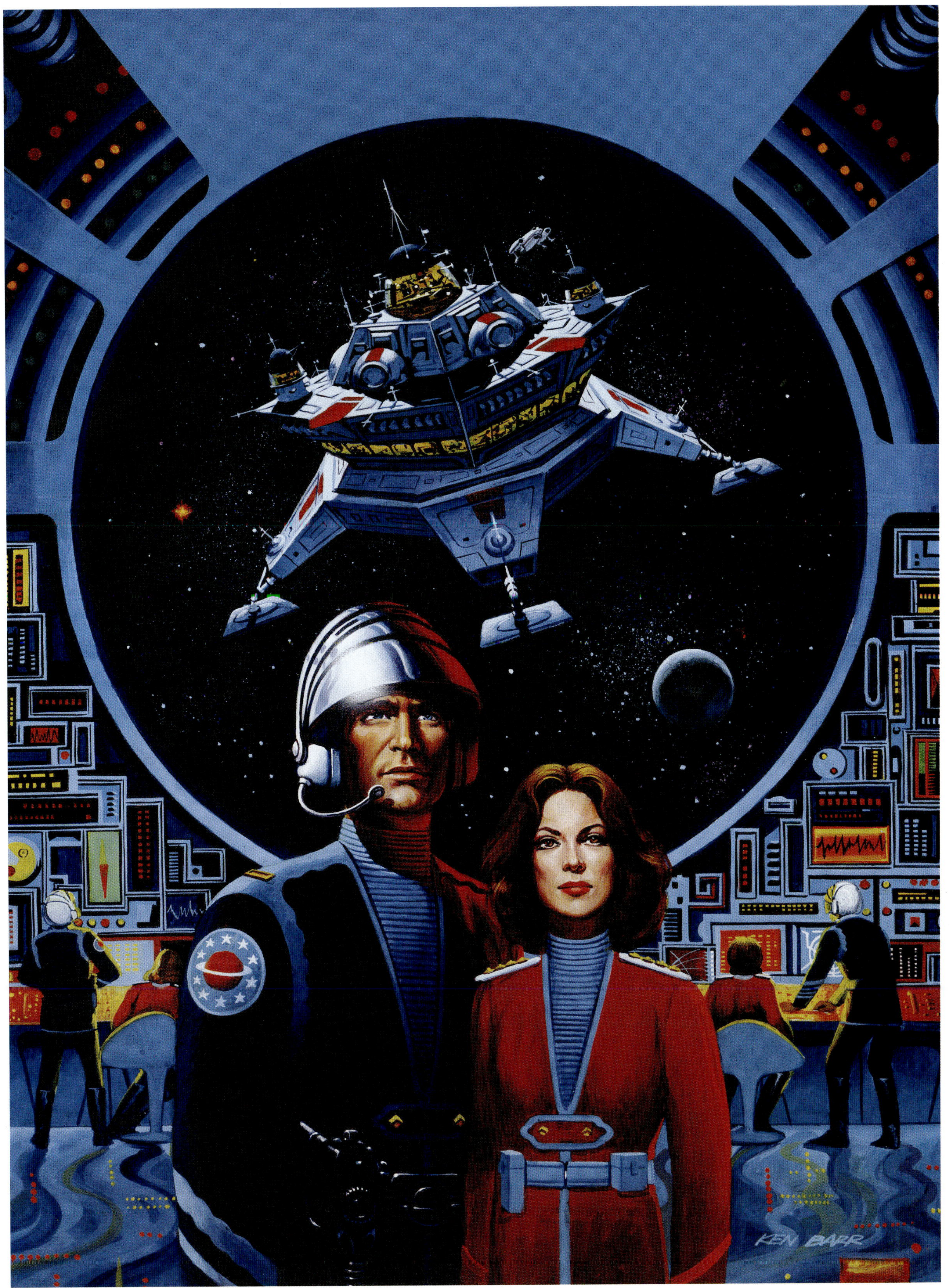
KEN BARR

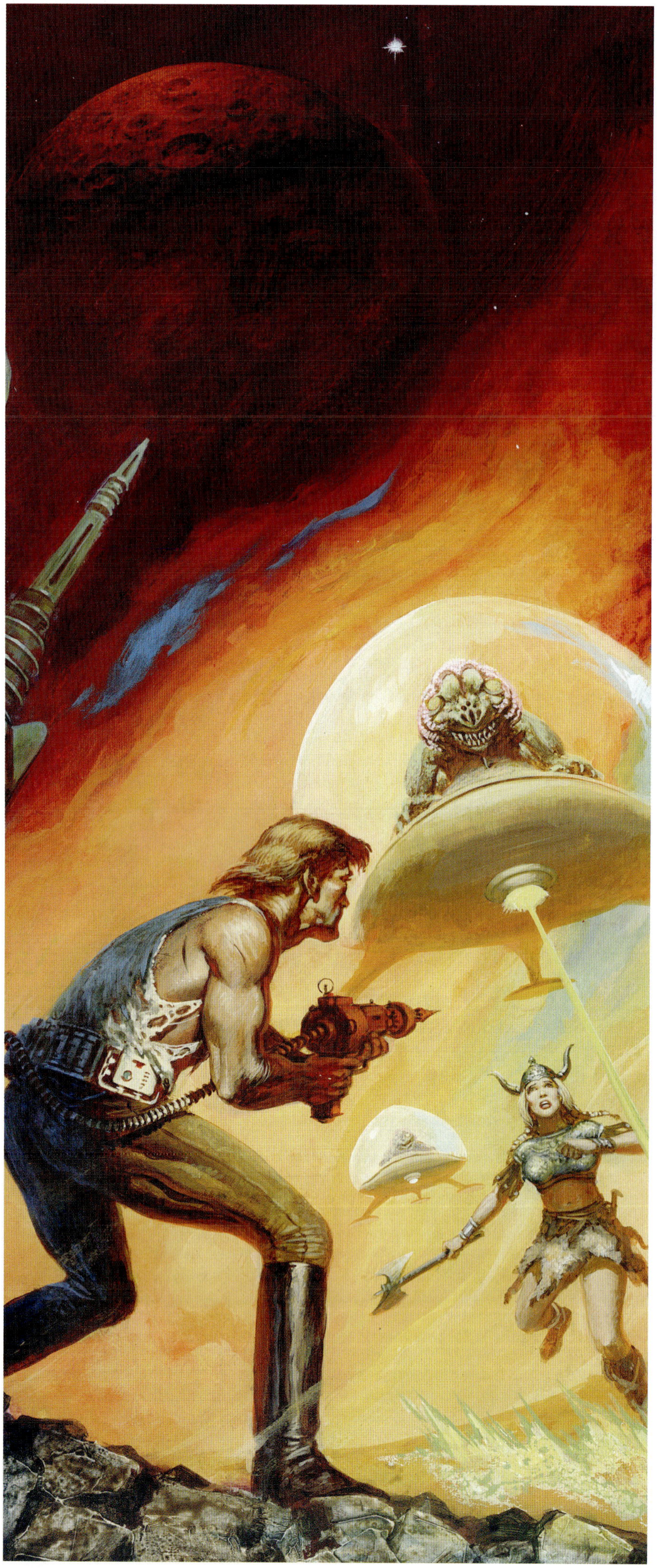

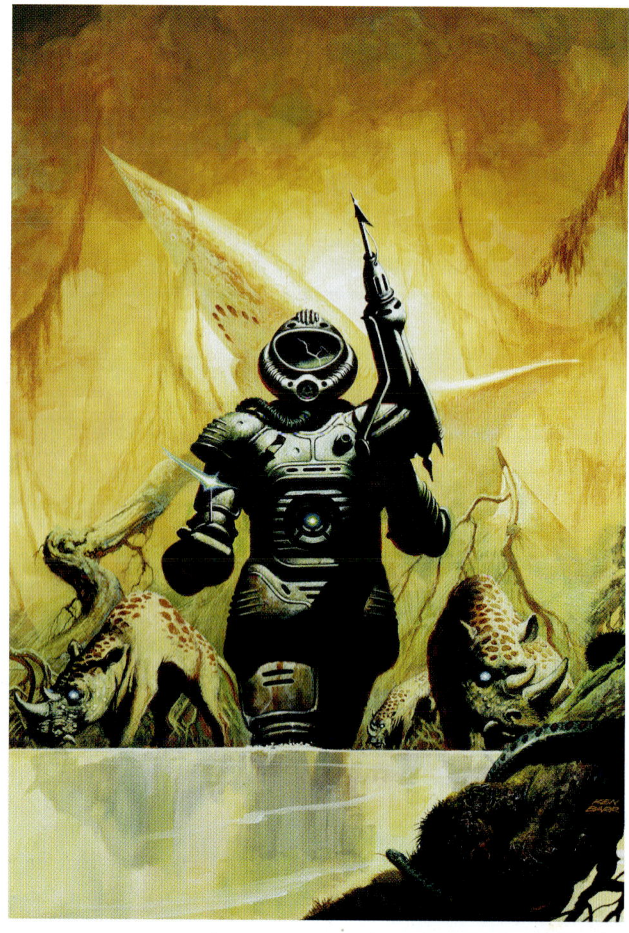

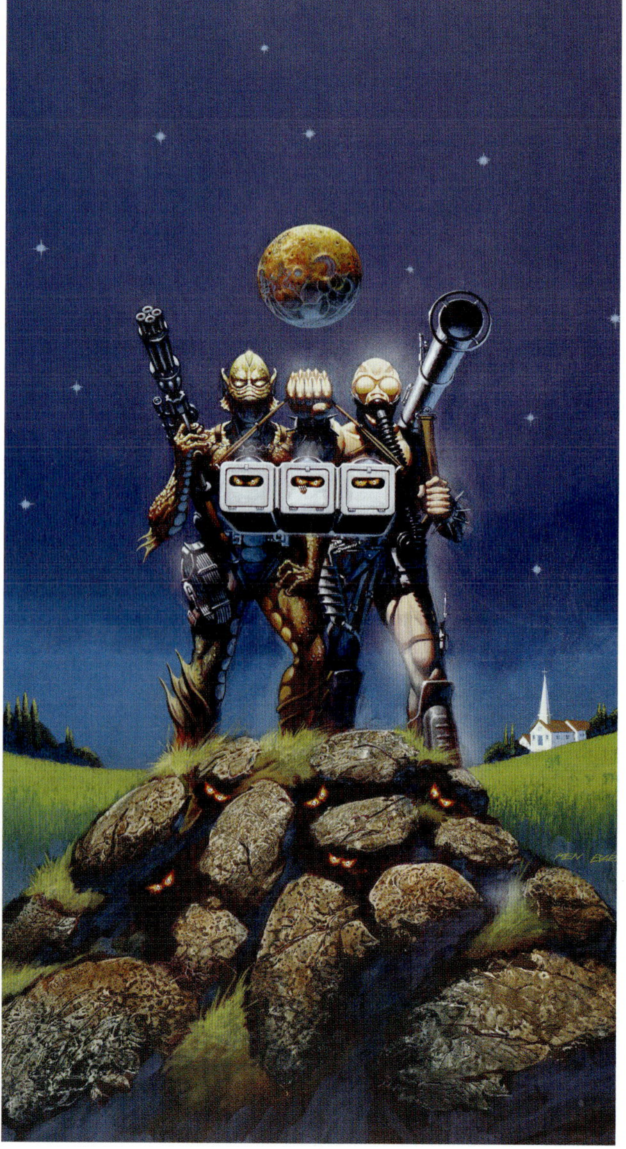

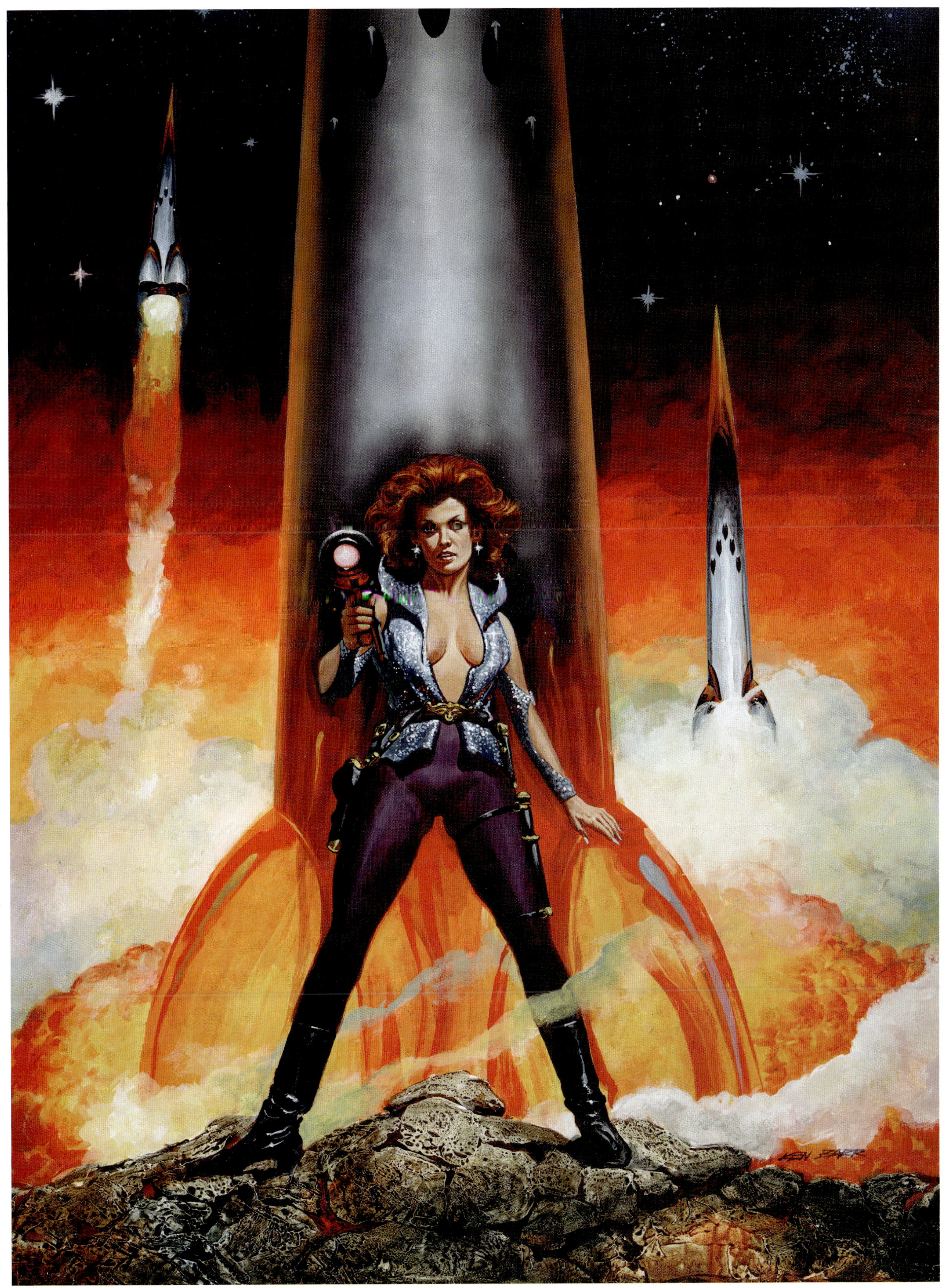
KEN BARR

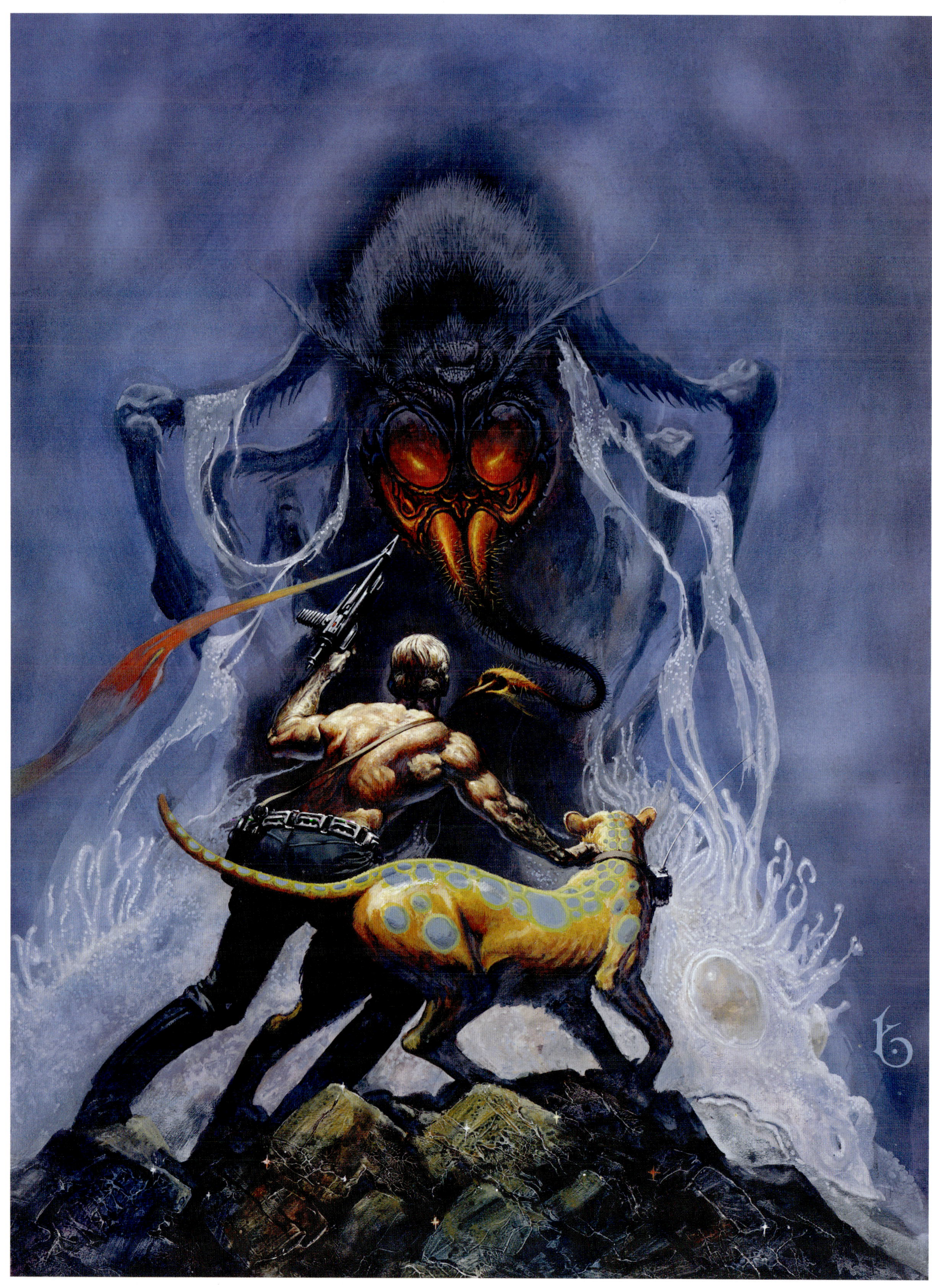

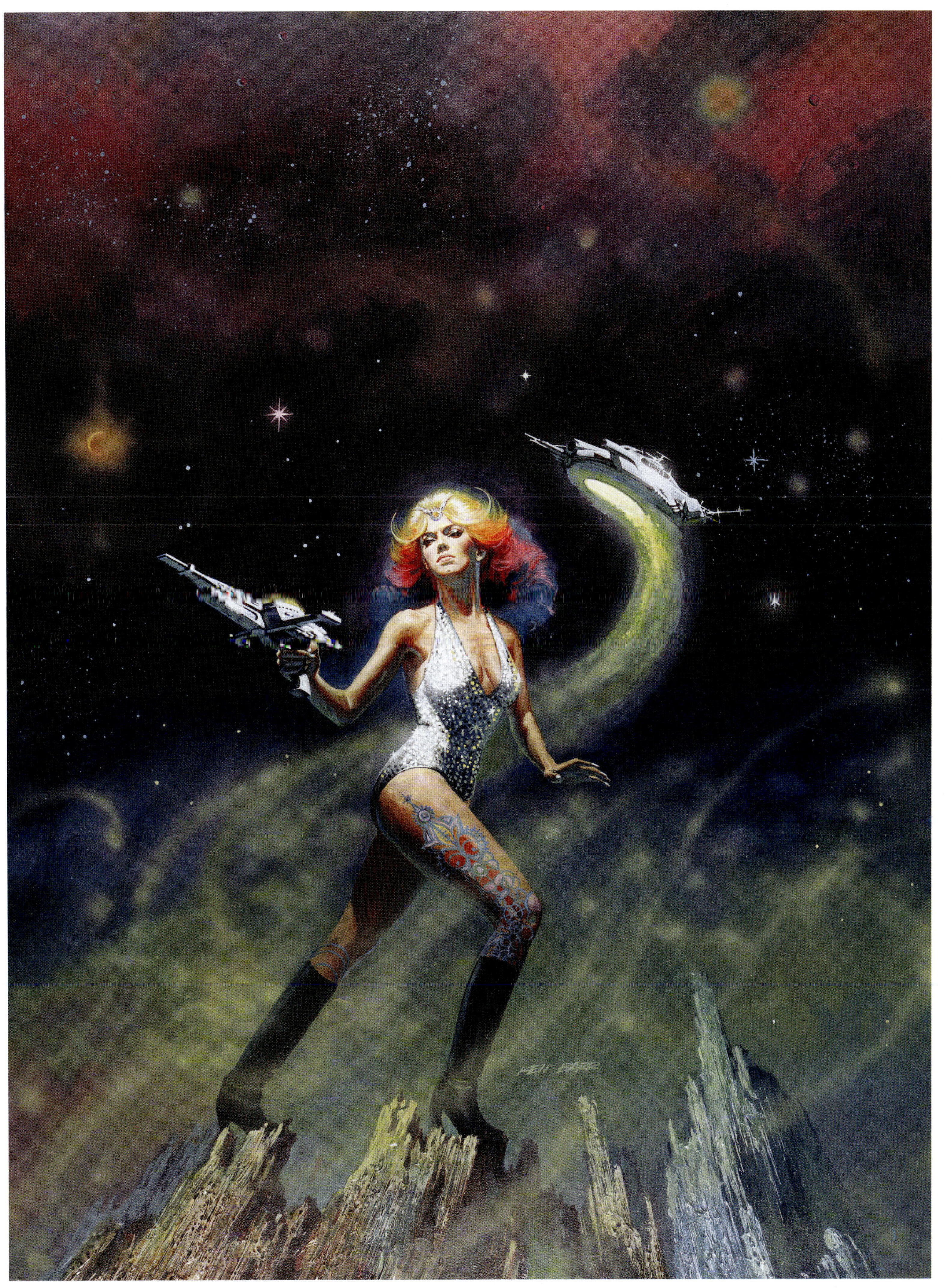
KEN BARR

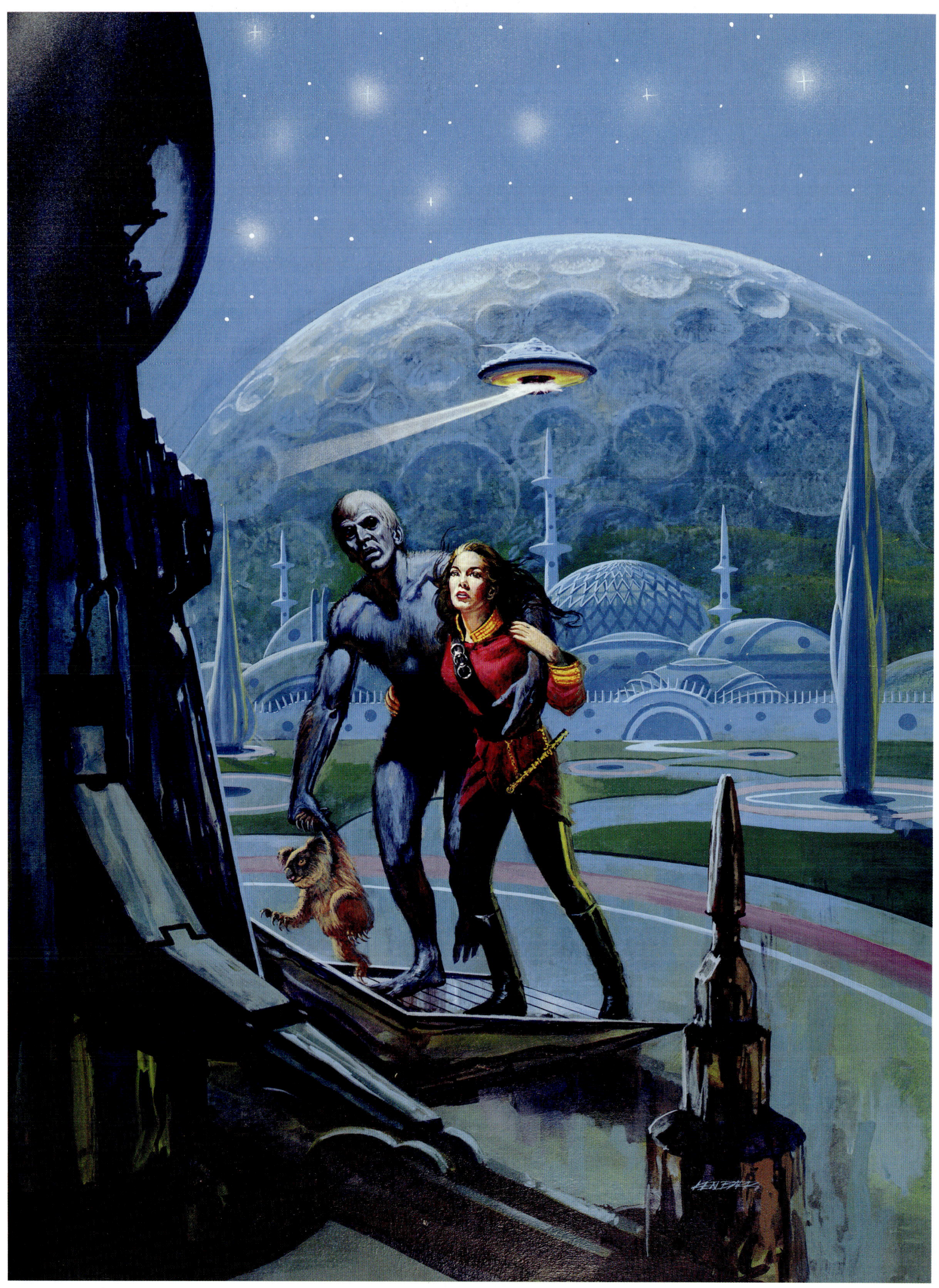

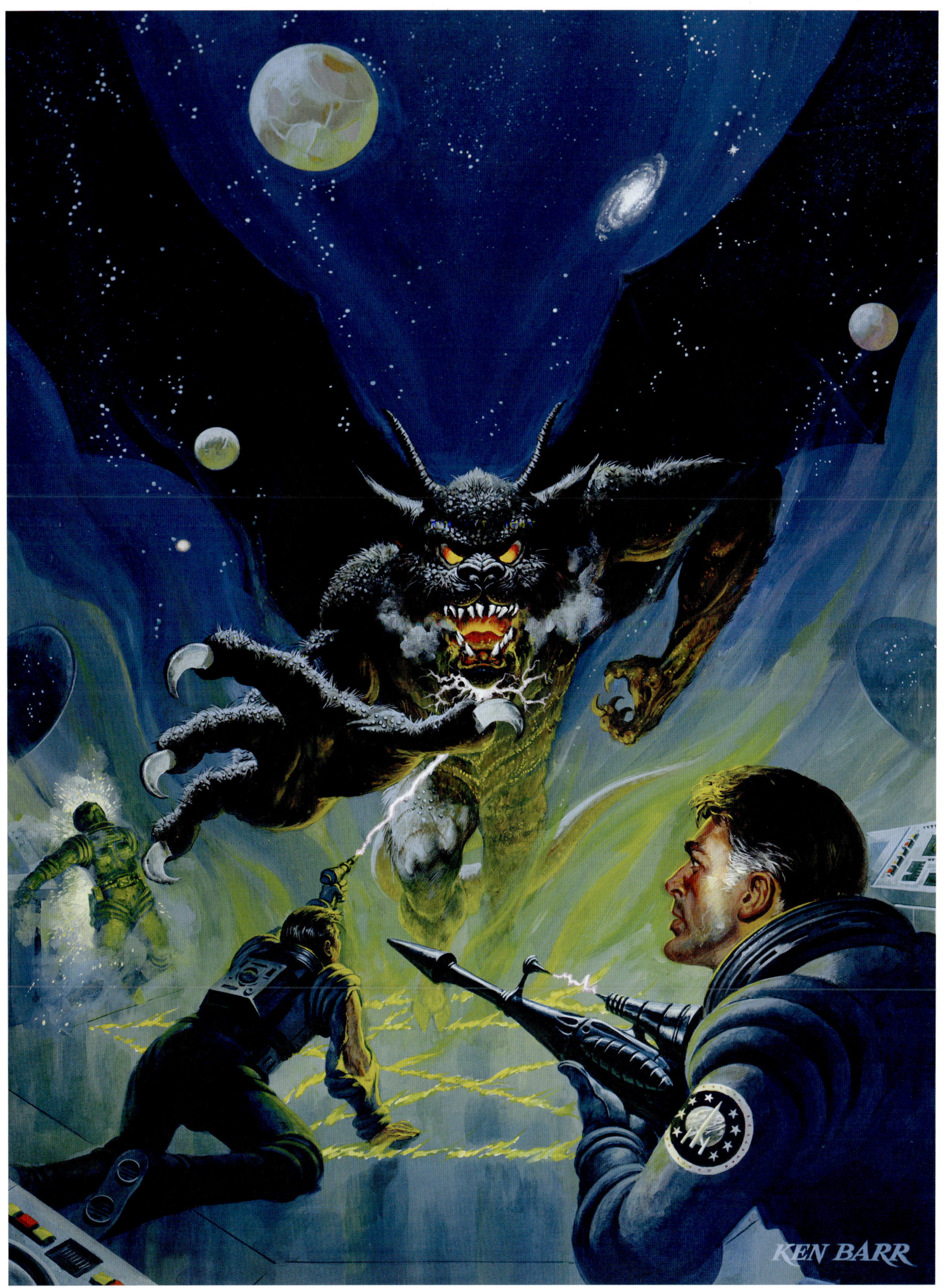
KEN BARR

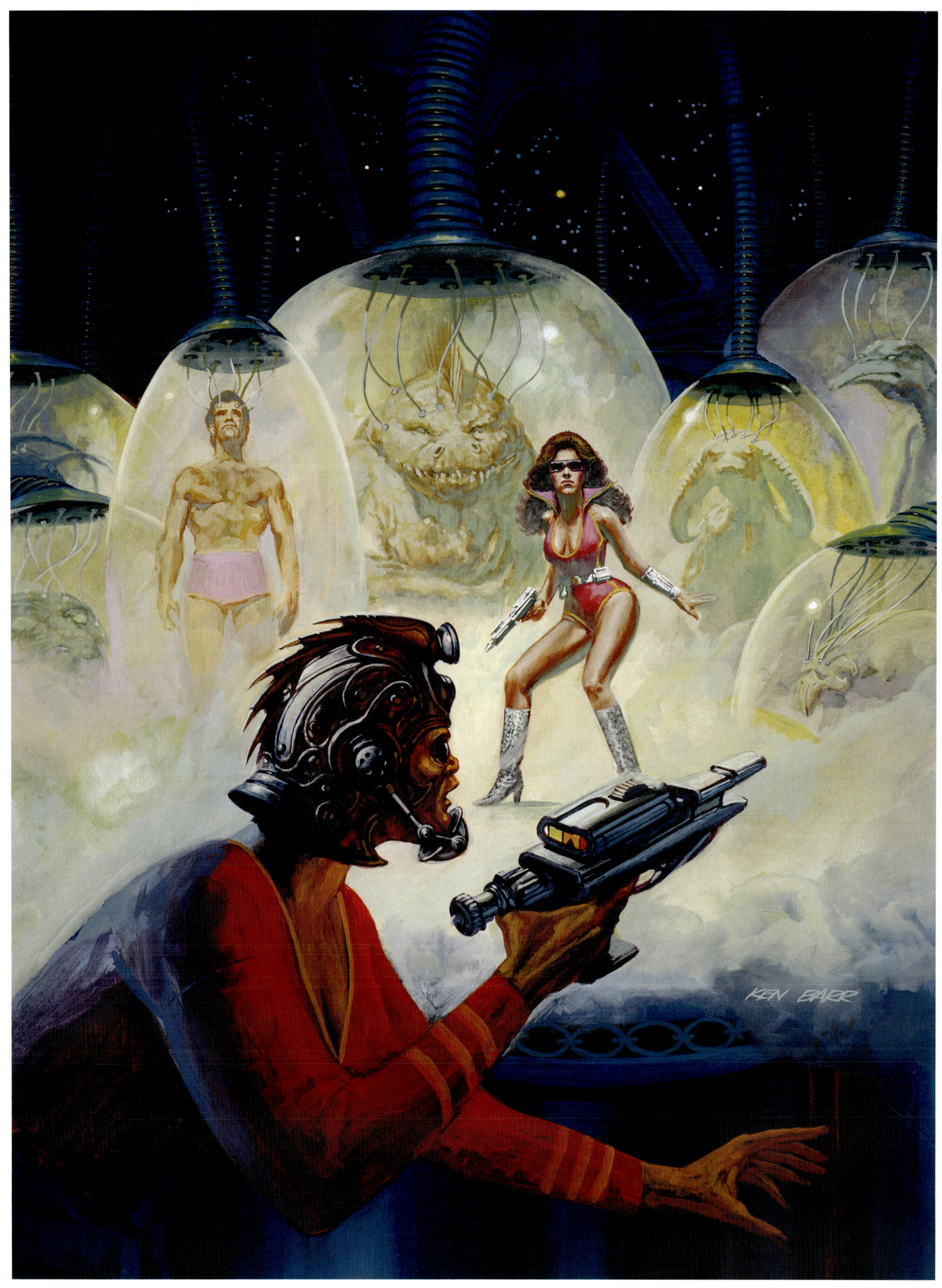
KEN BARR

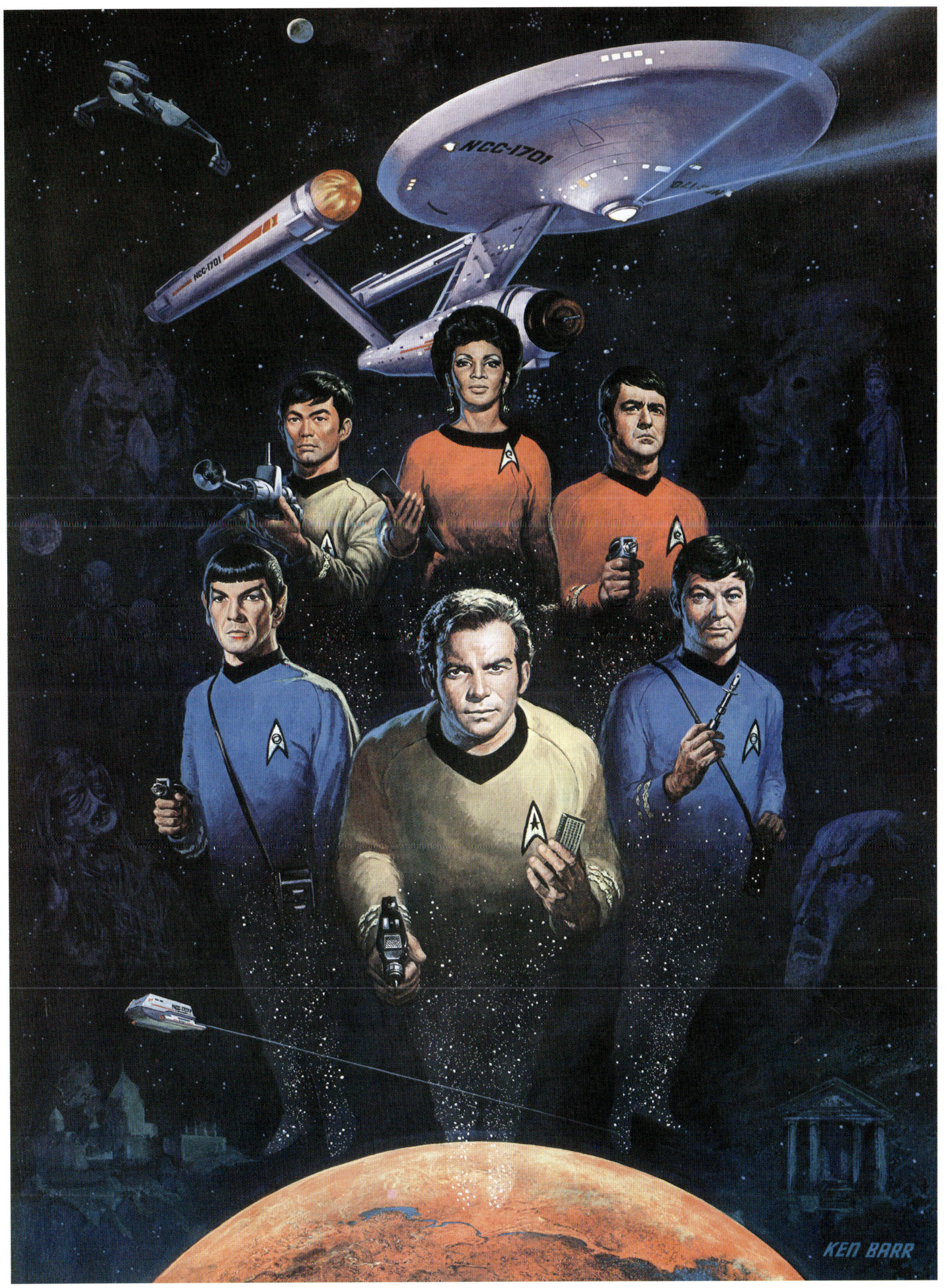
NCC-1701
NCC-1701
KEN BARR

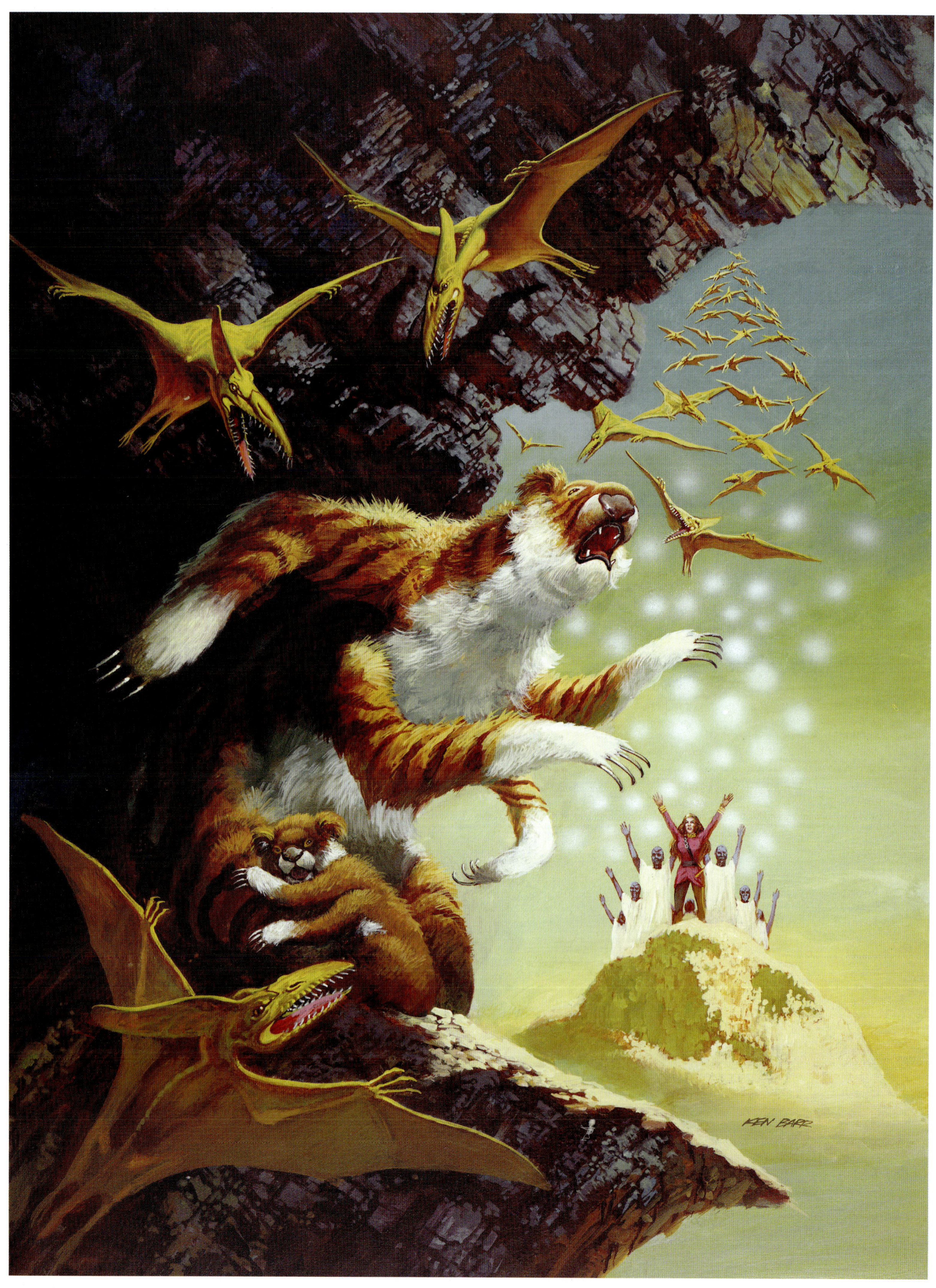
KEN BARR

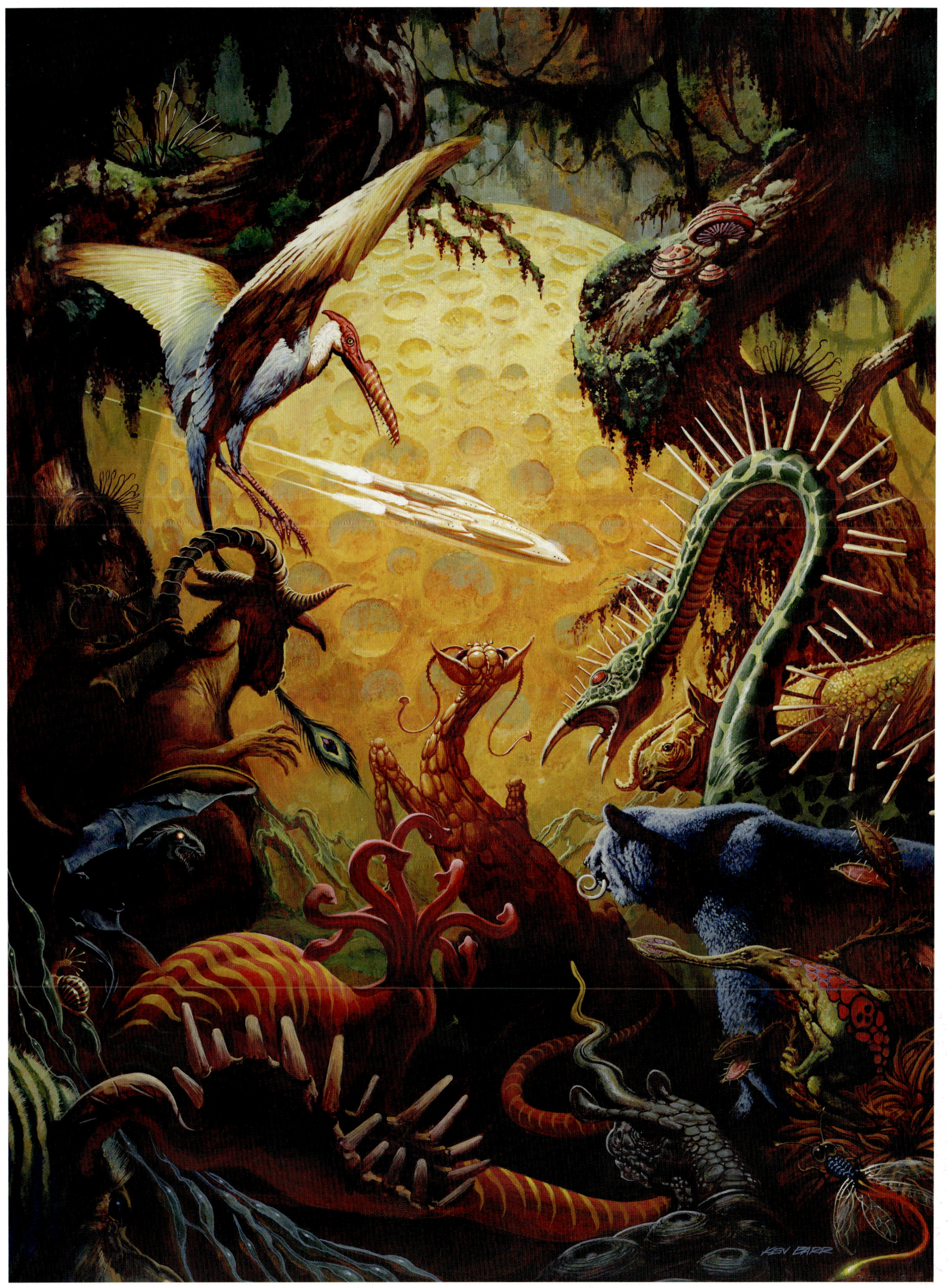
KEN BARR

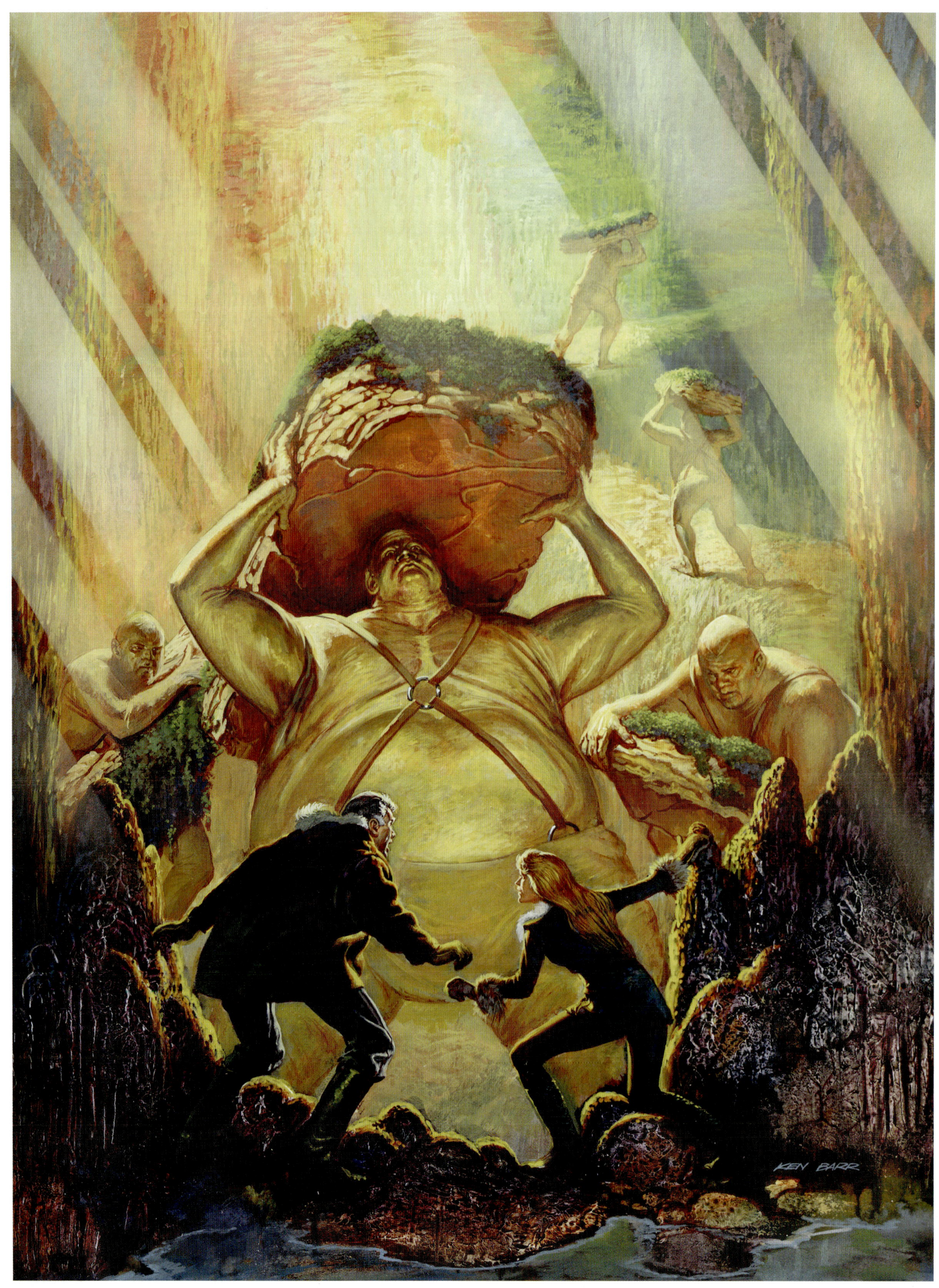
KEN BARR

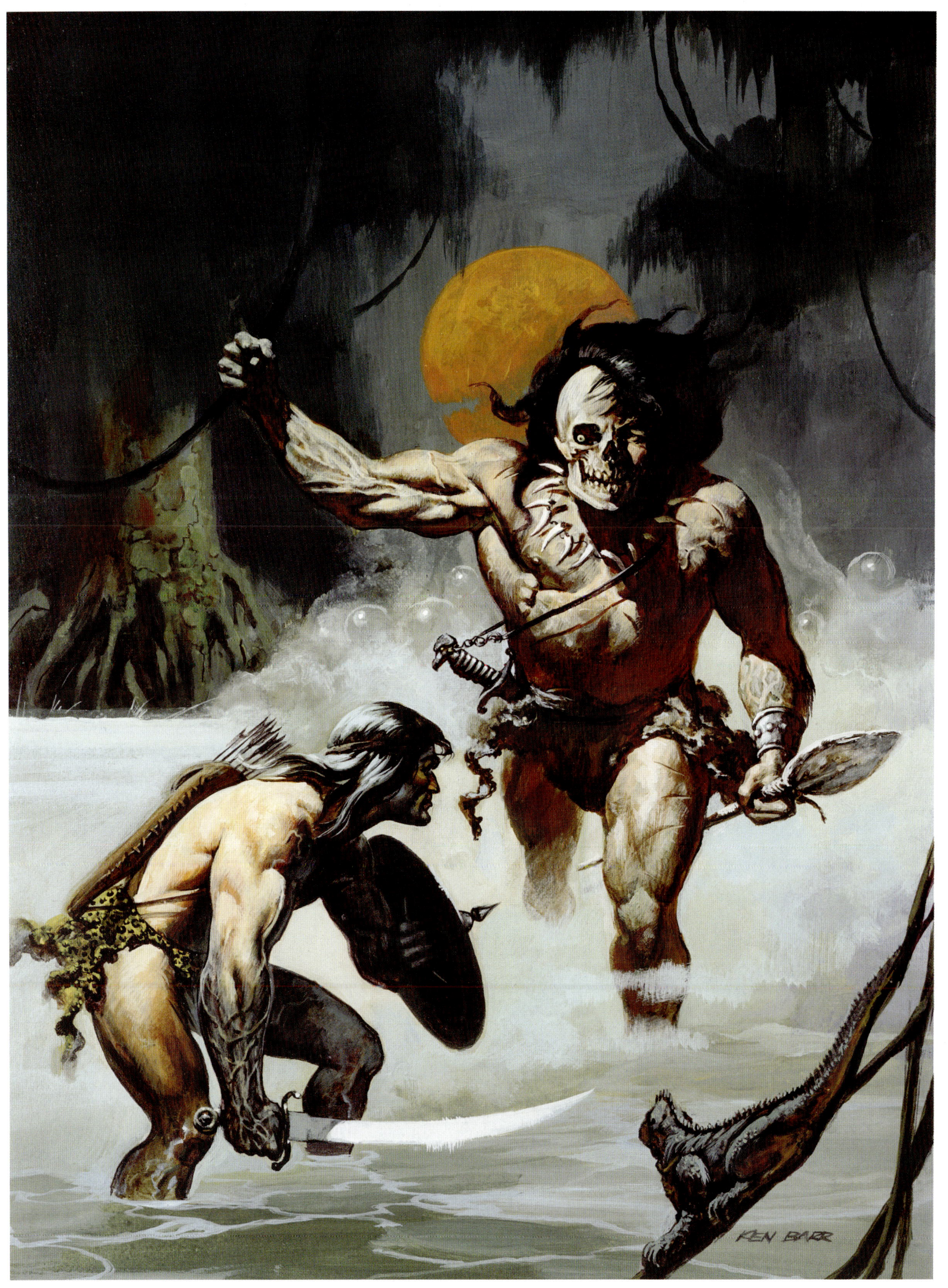
KEN BARR

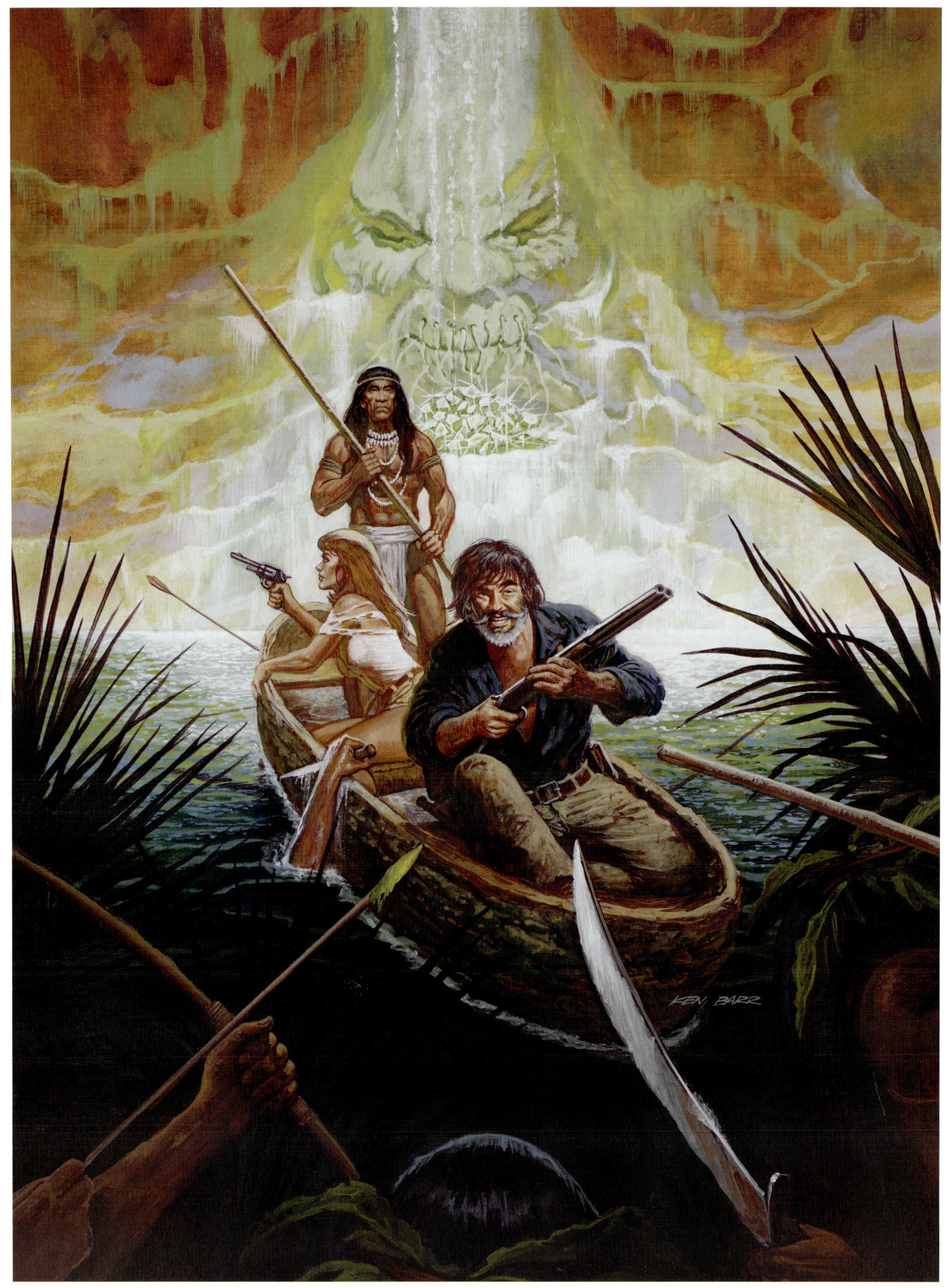
KEN BARR

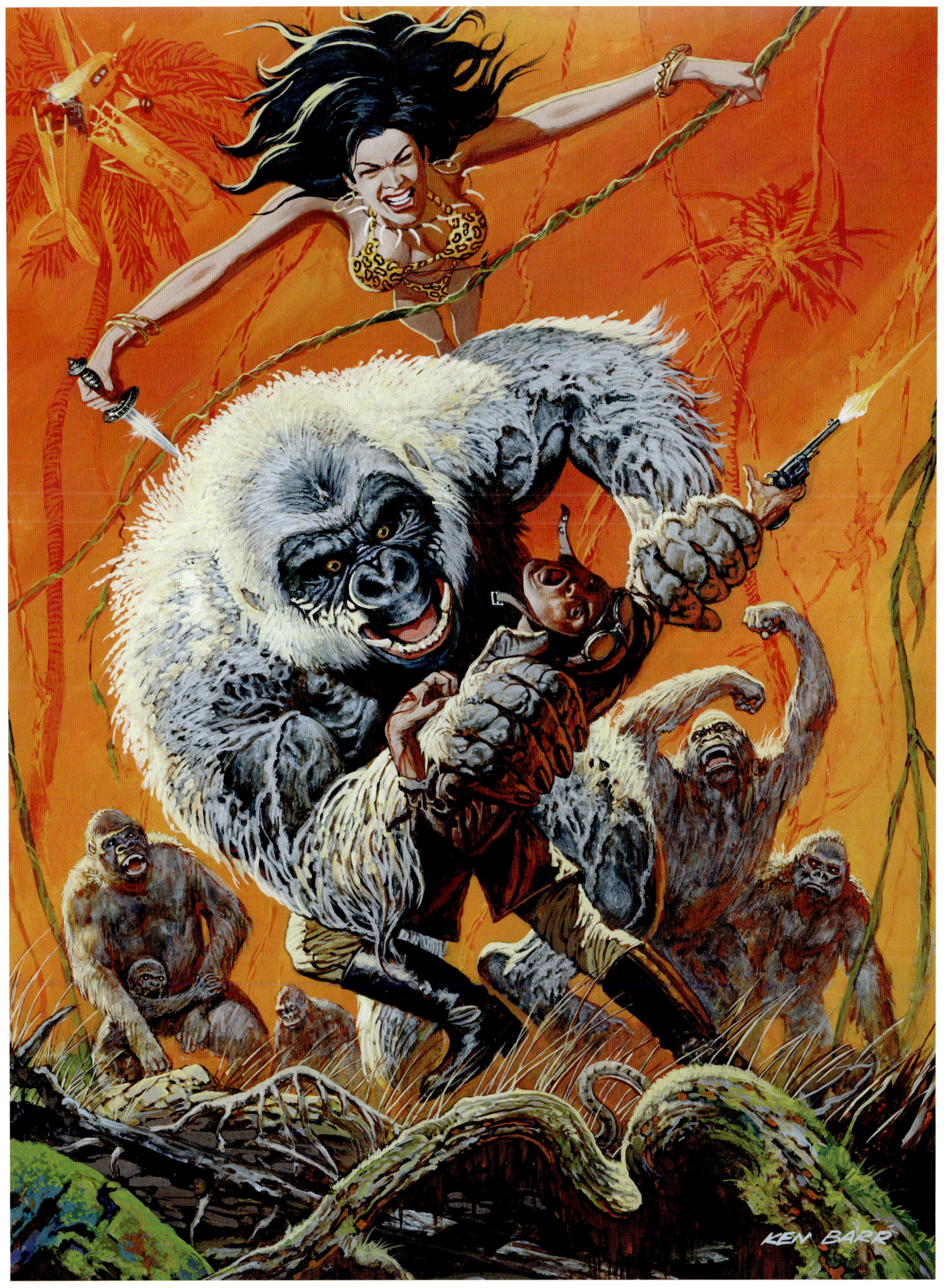
KEN BARR

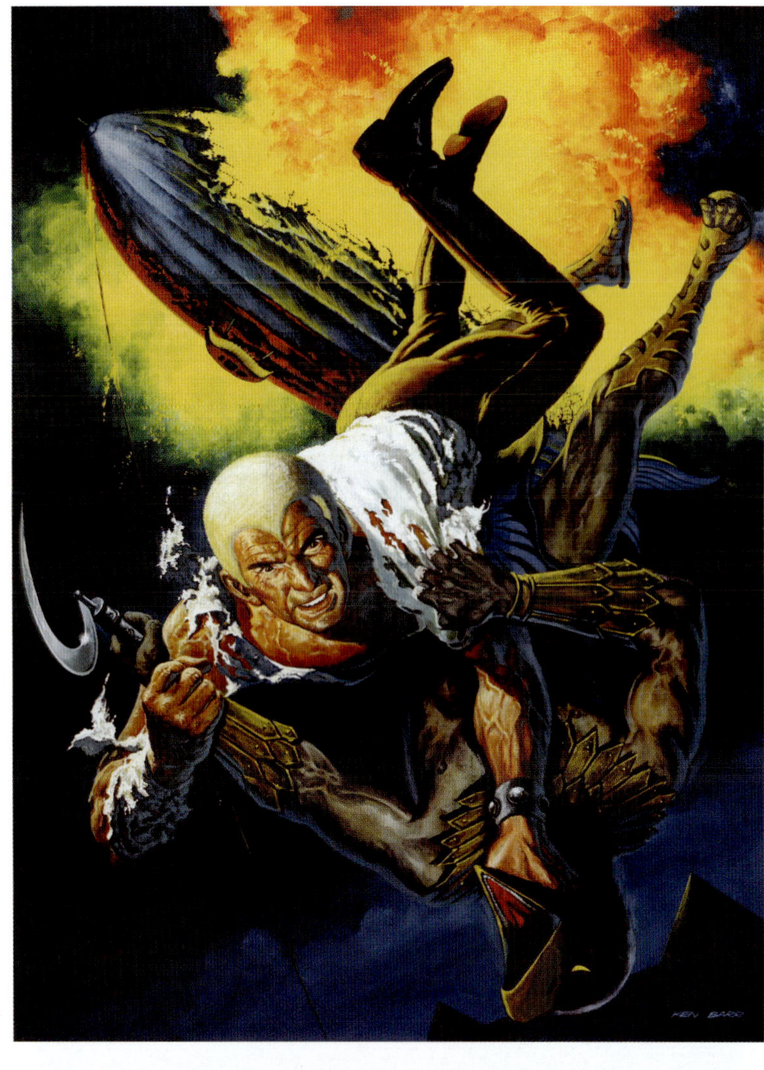
KEN BARR

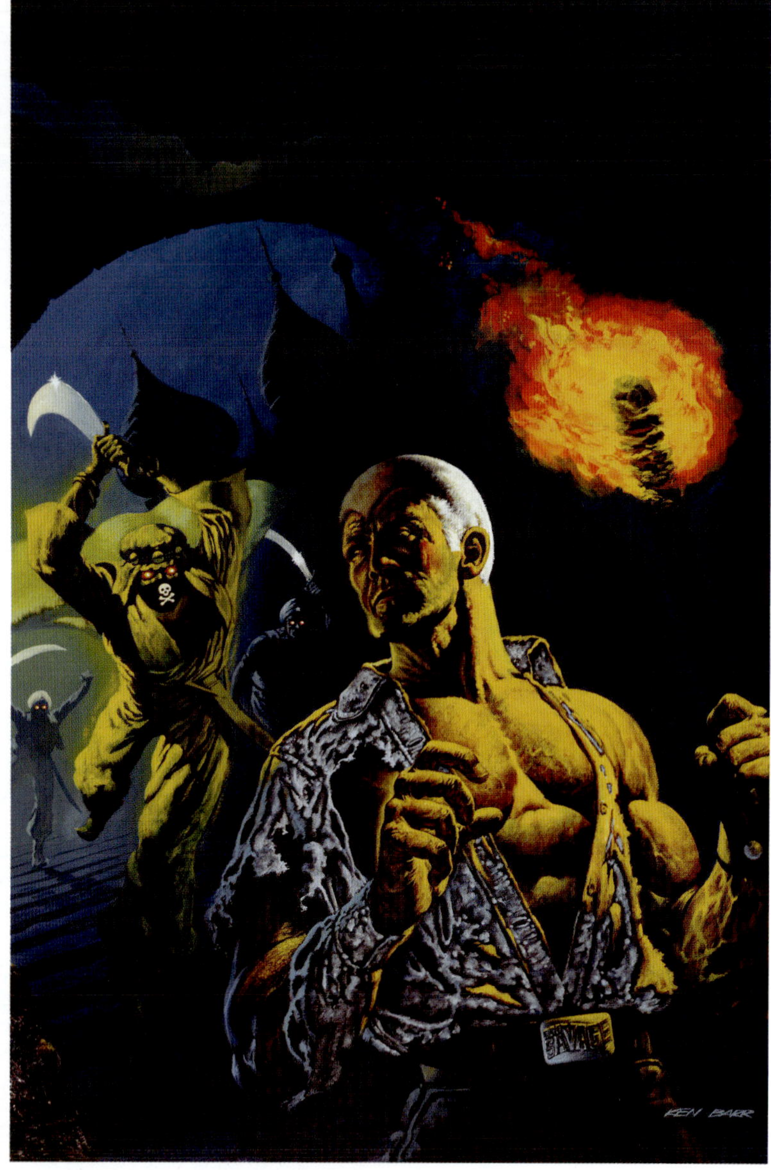
KEN BARR

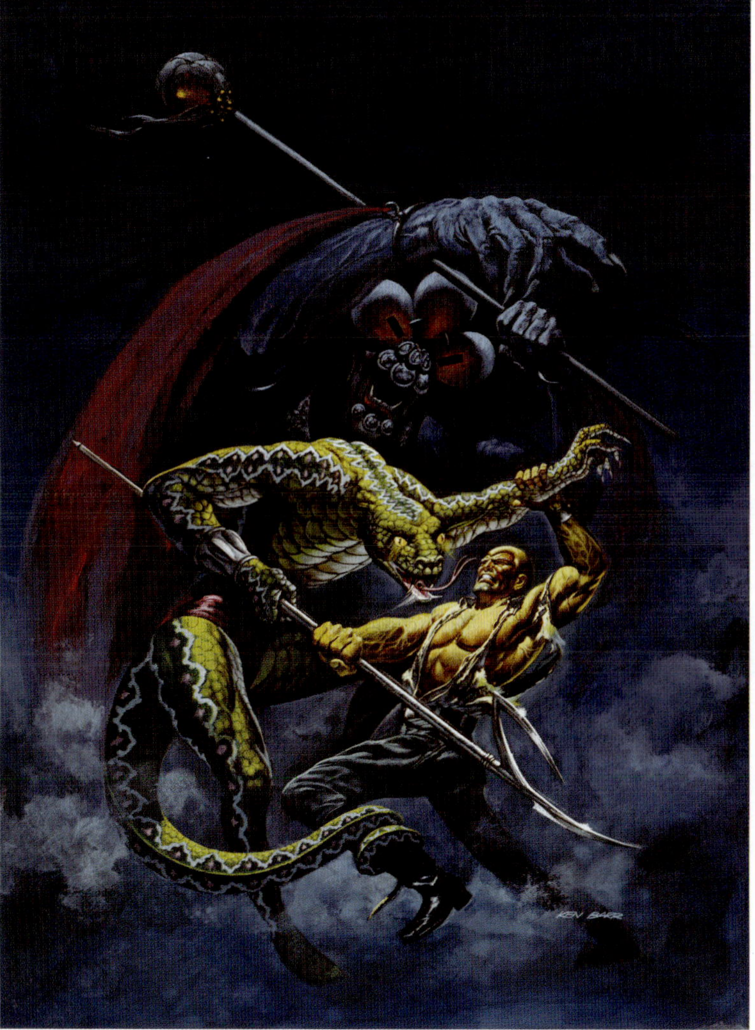
KEN BARR

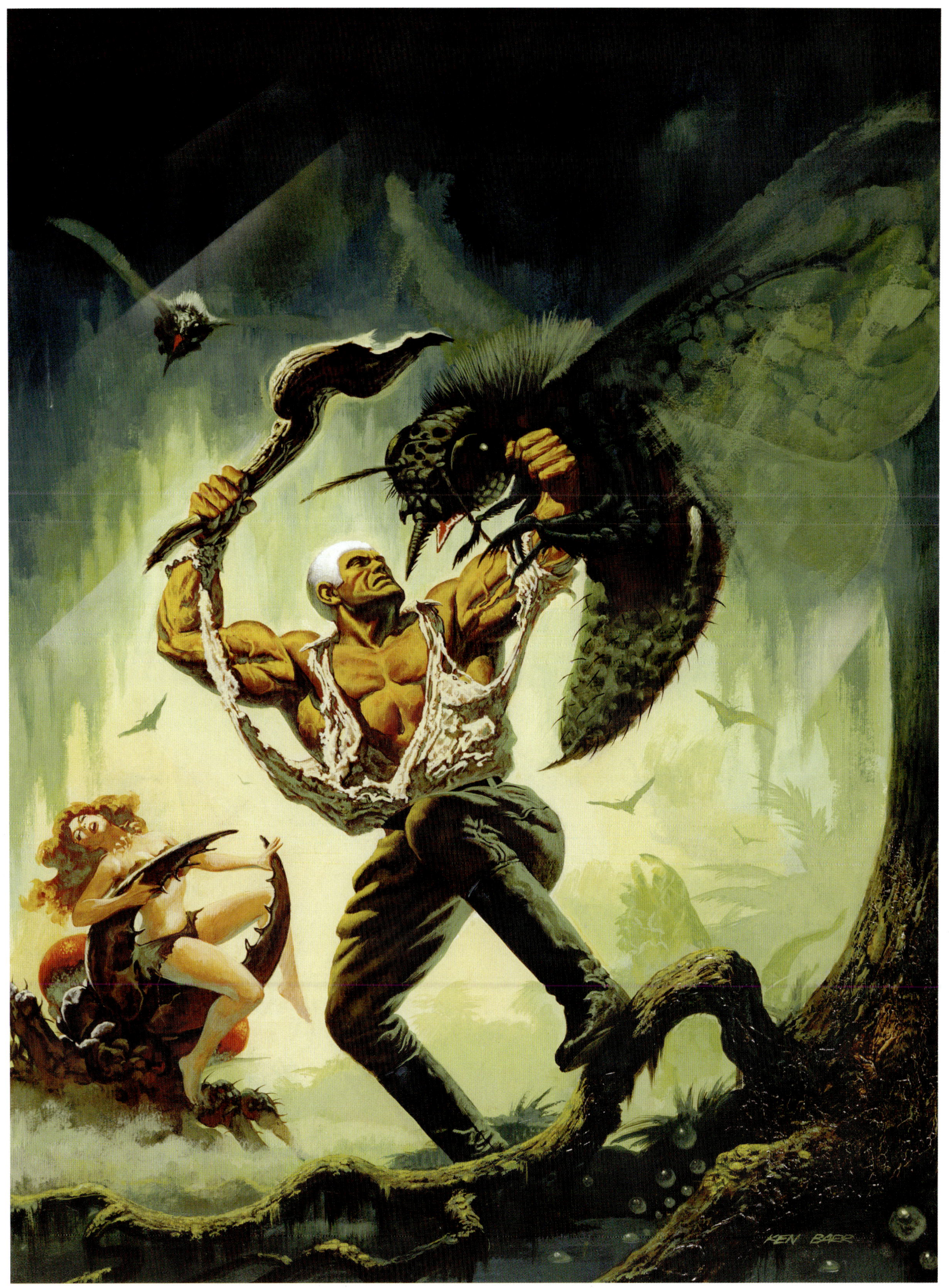
KEN BARR

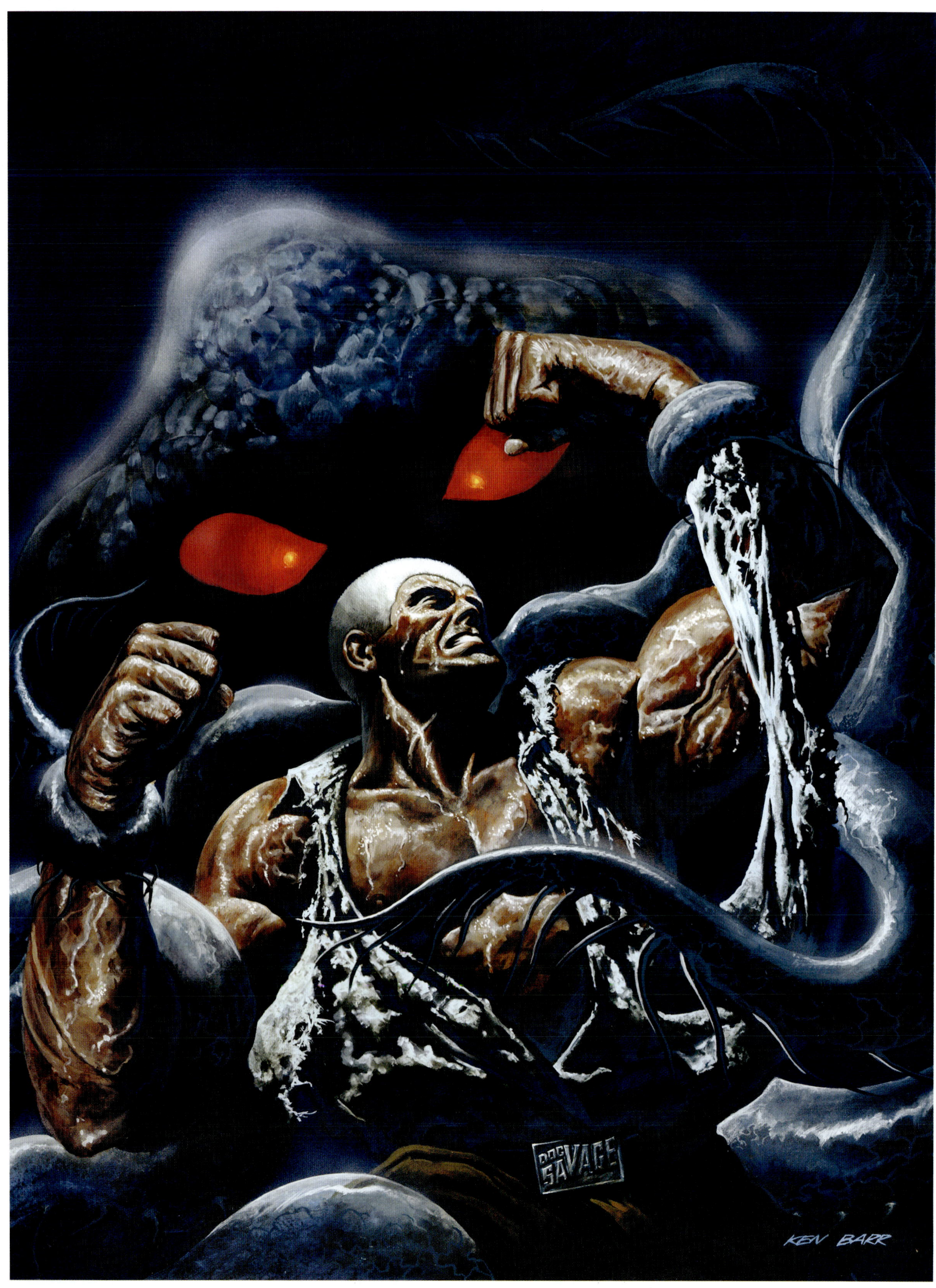
DOC SAVAGE
KEN BARR

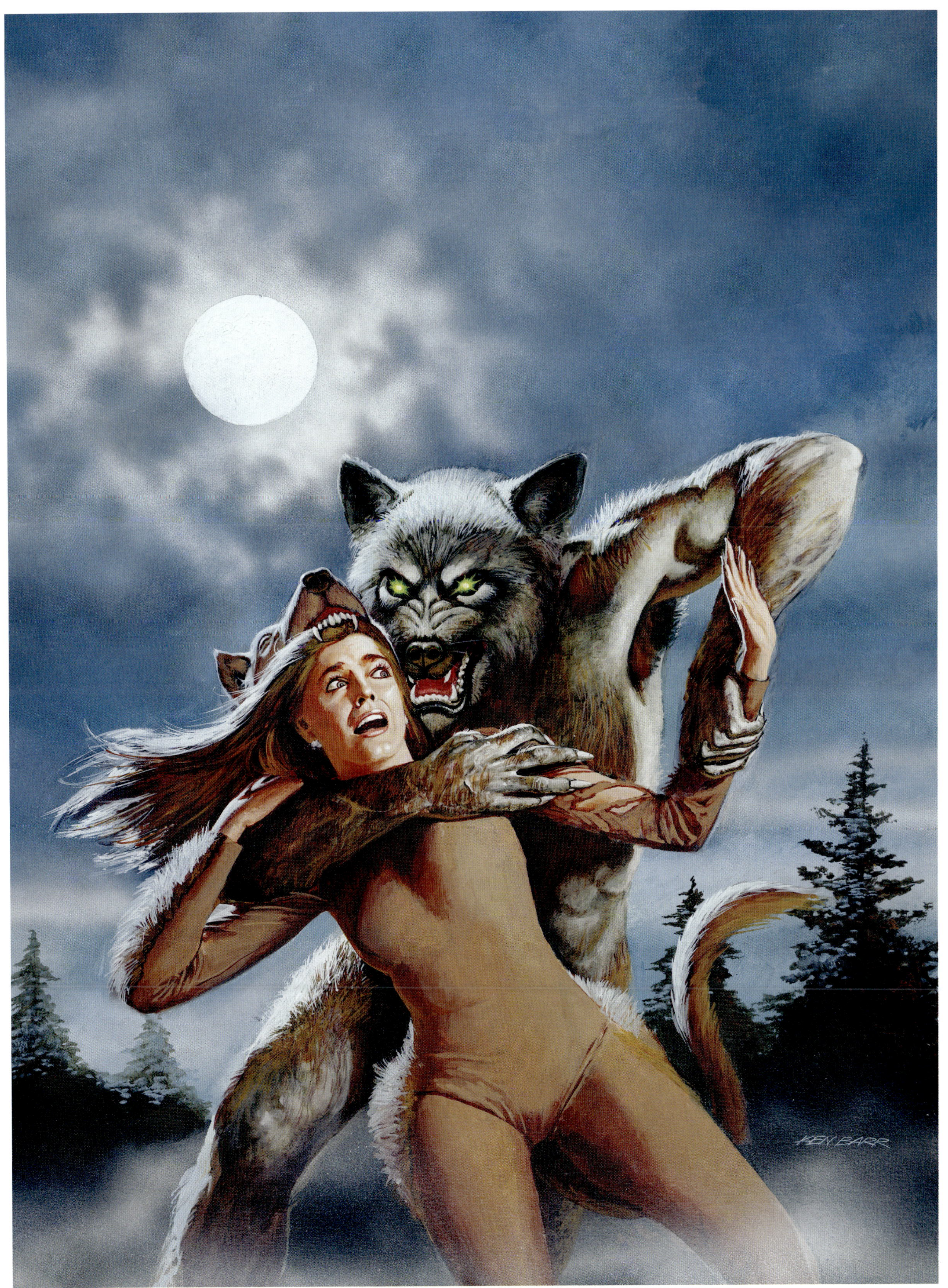
KEN BARR

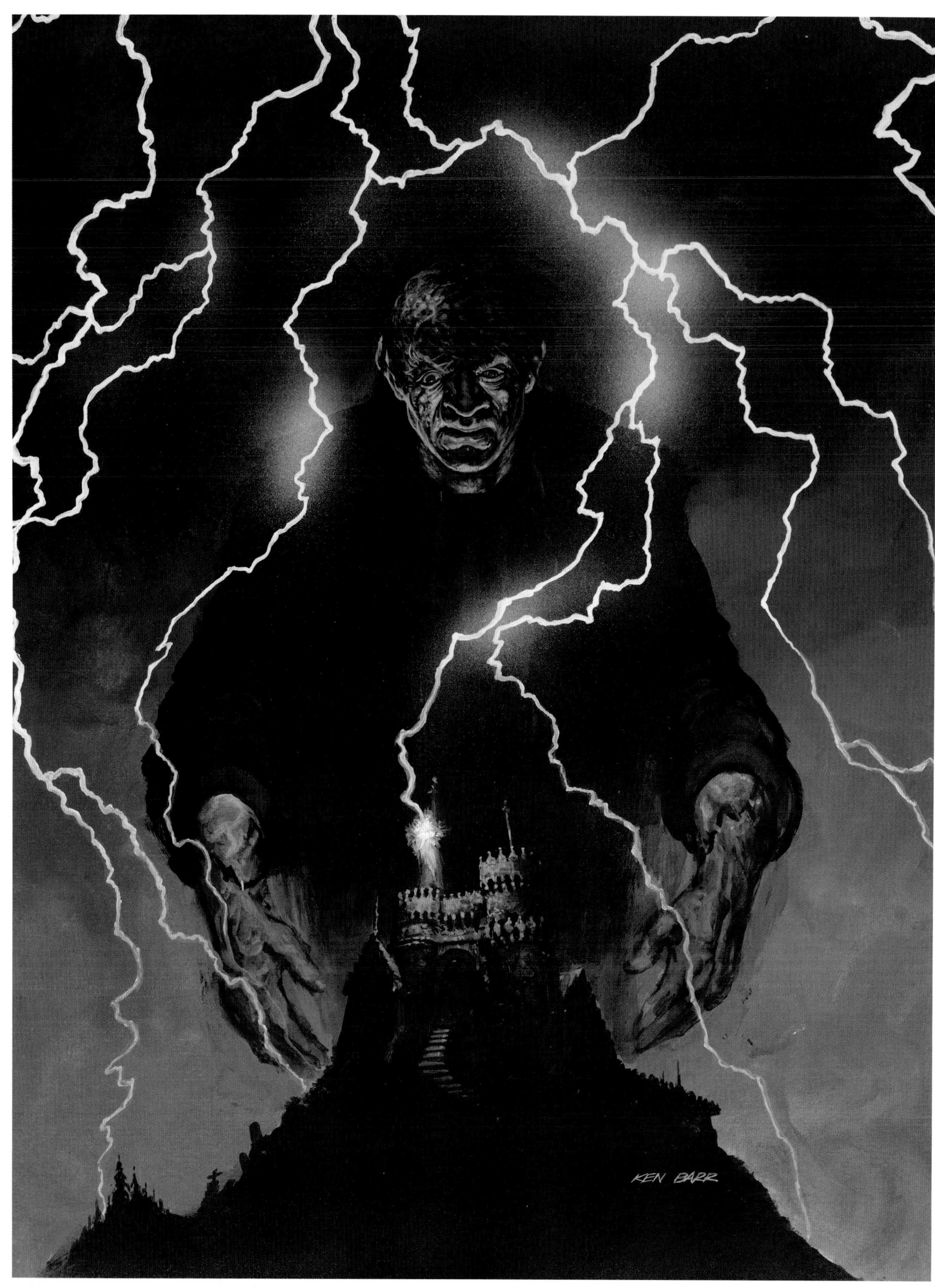
KEN BARR

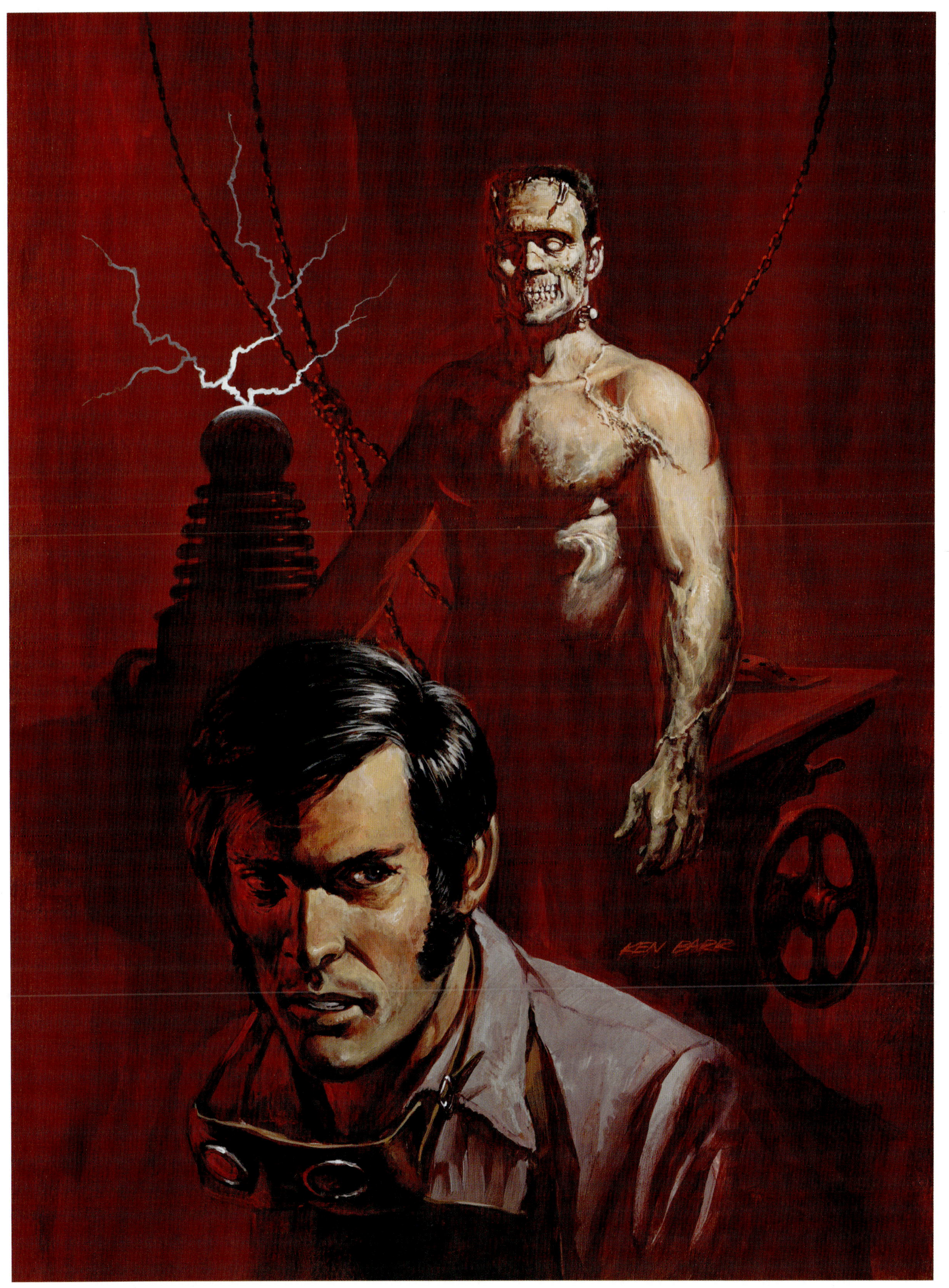
KEN BARR

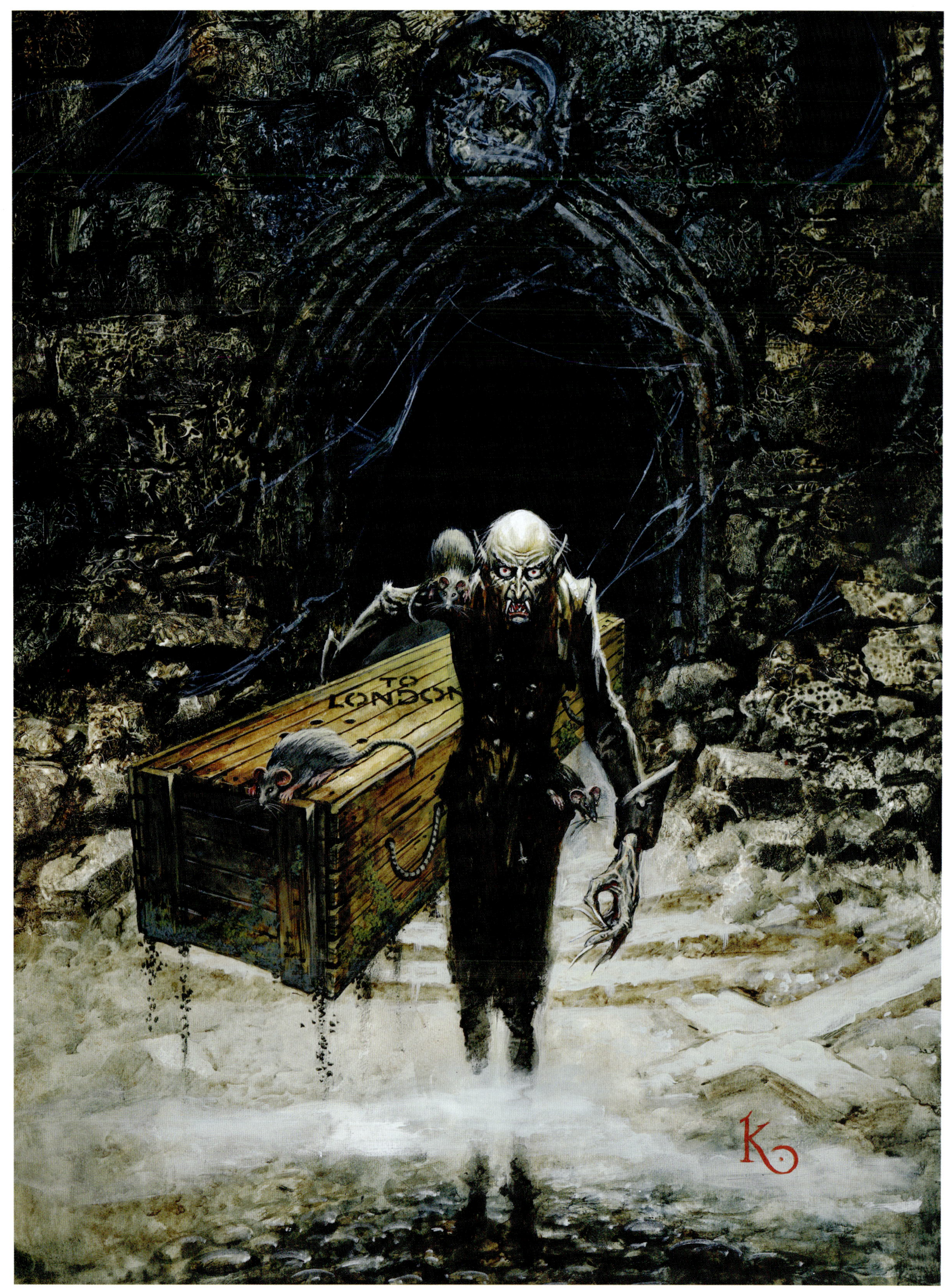
TO
LONDON

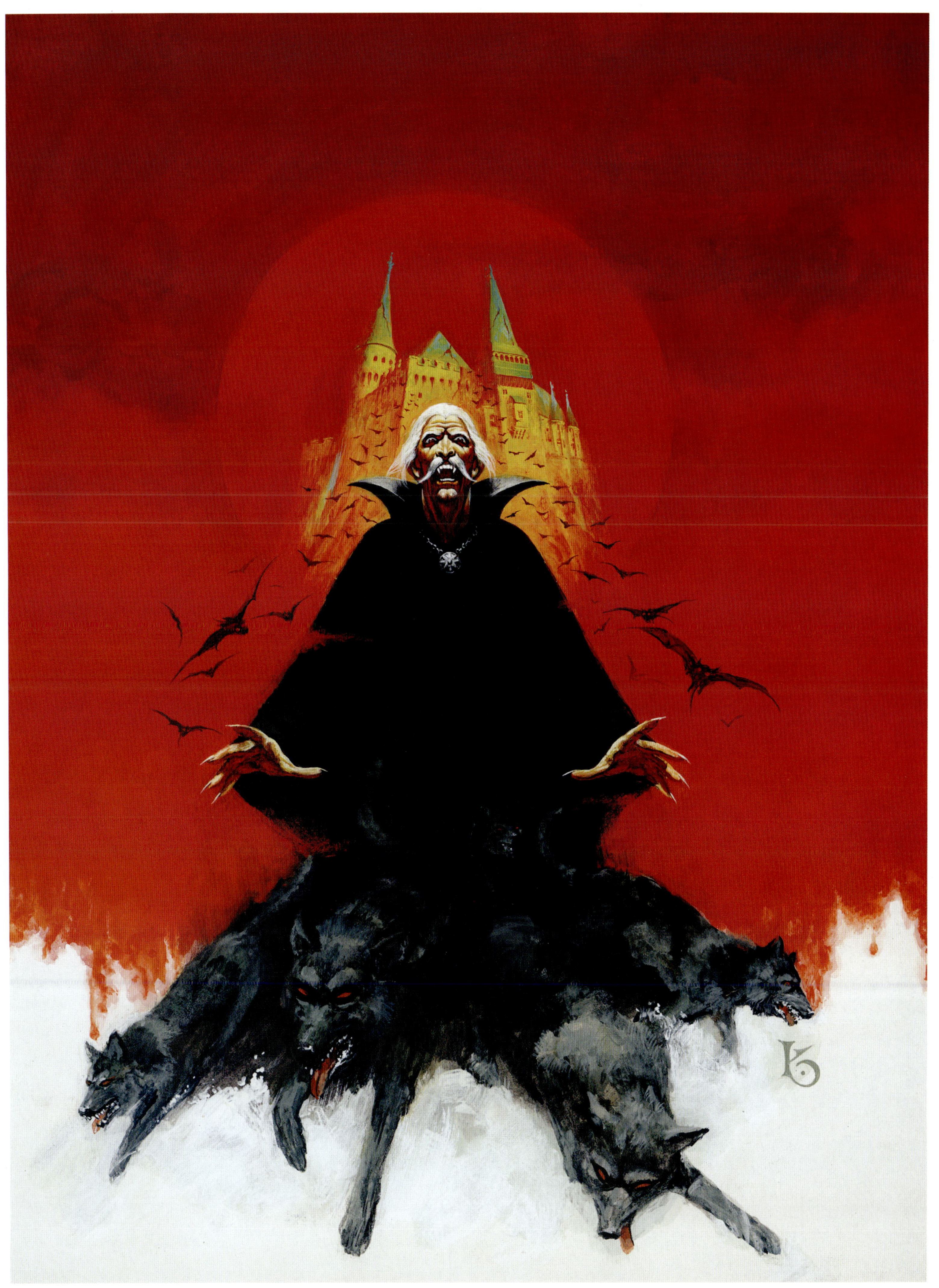

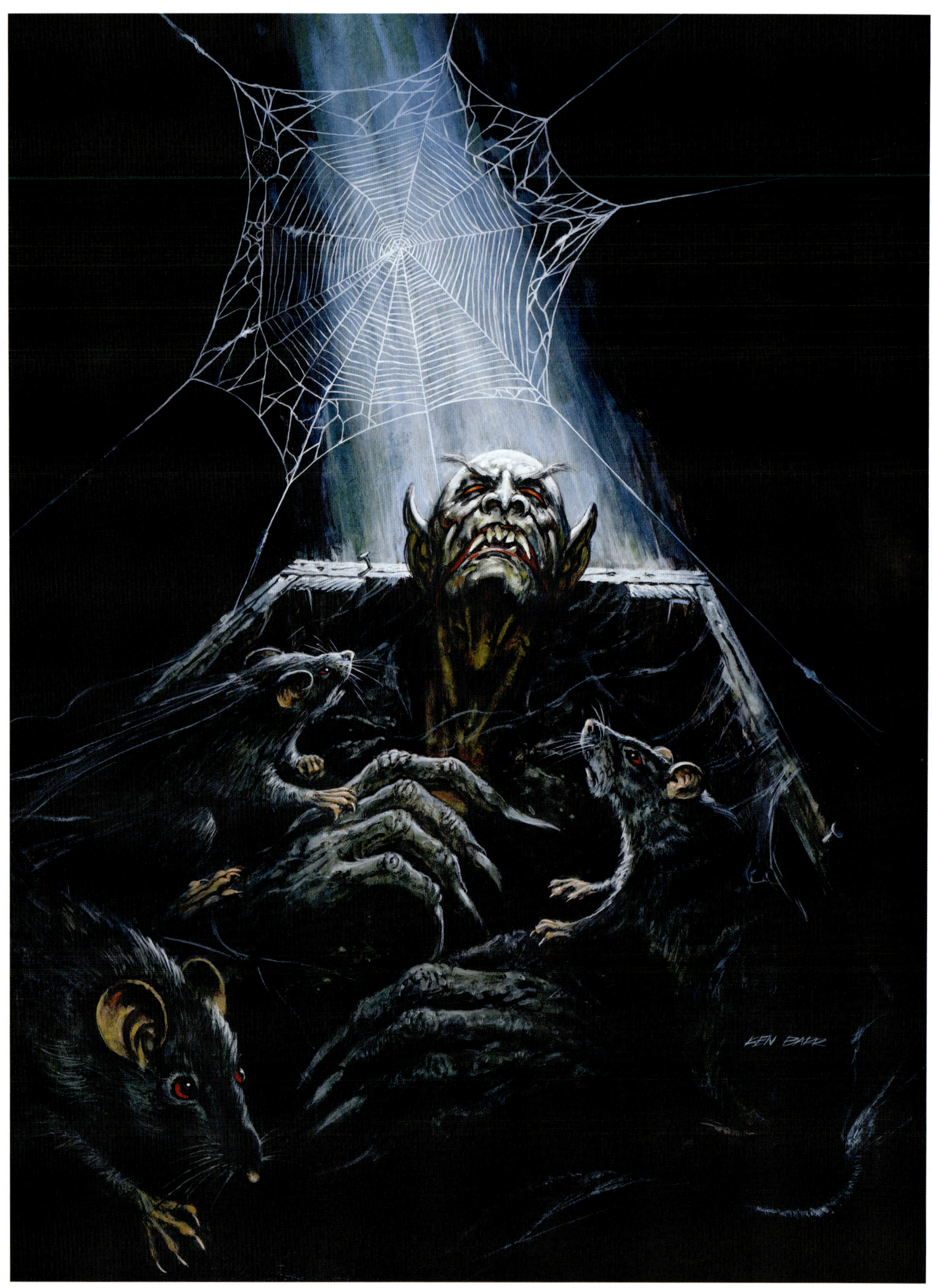
KEN BARR

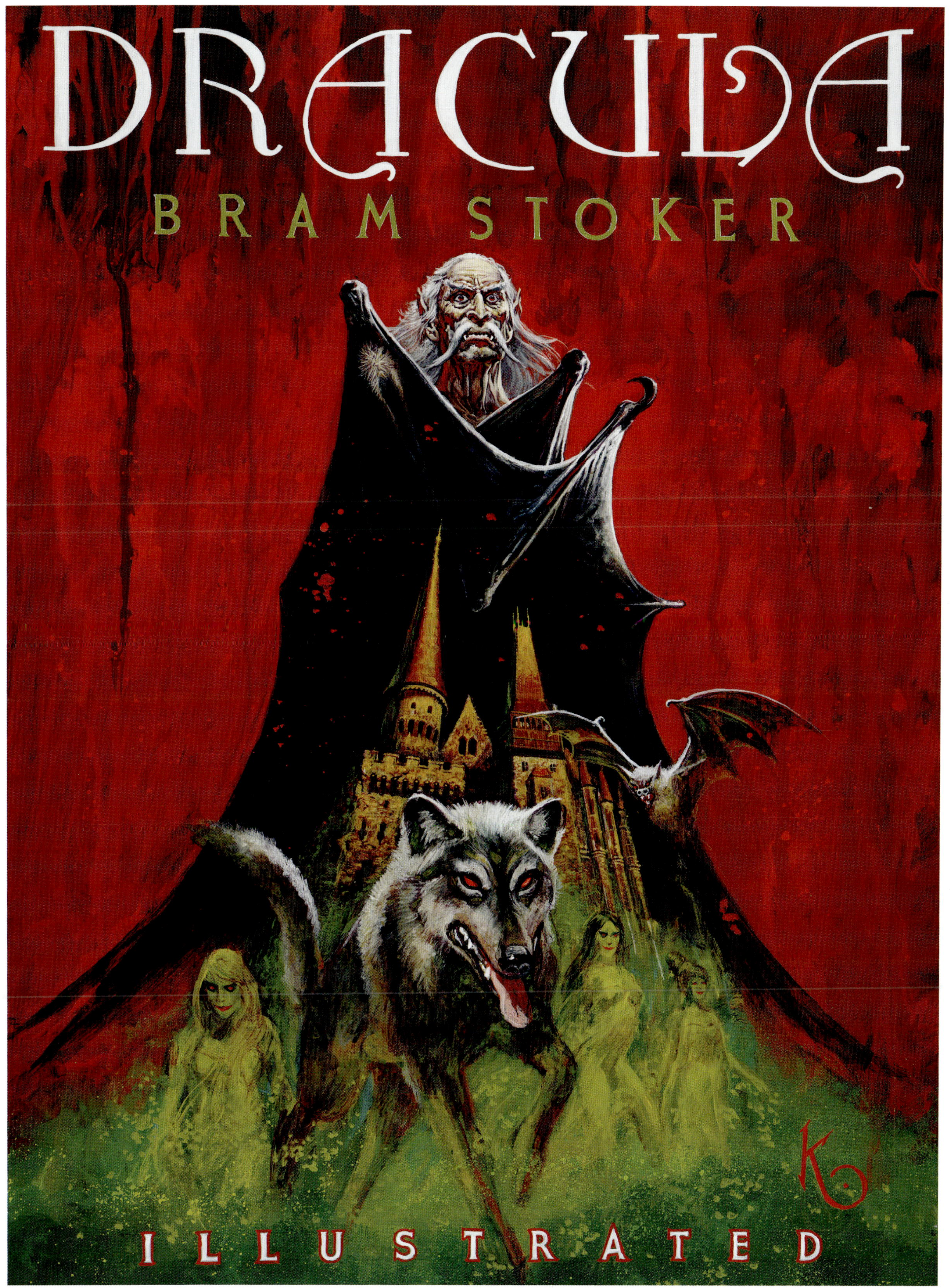
DRACULA
BRAM STOKER
ILLUSTRATED

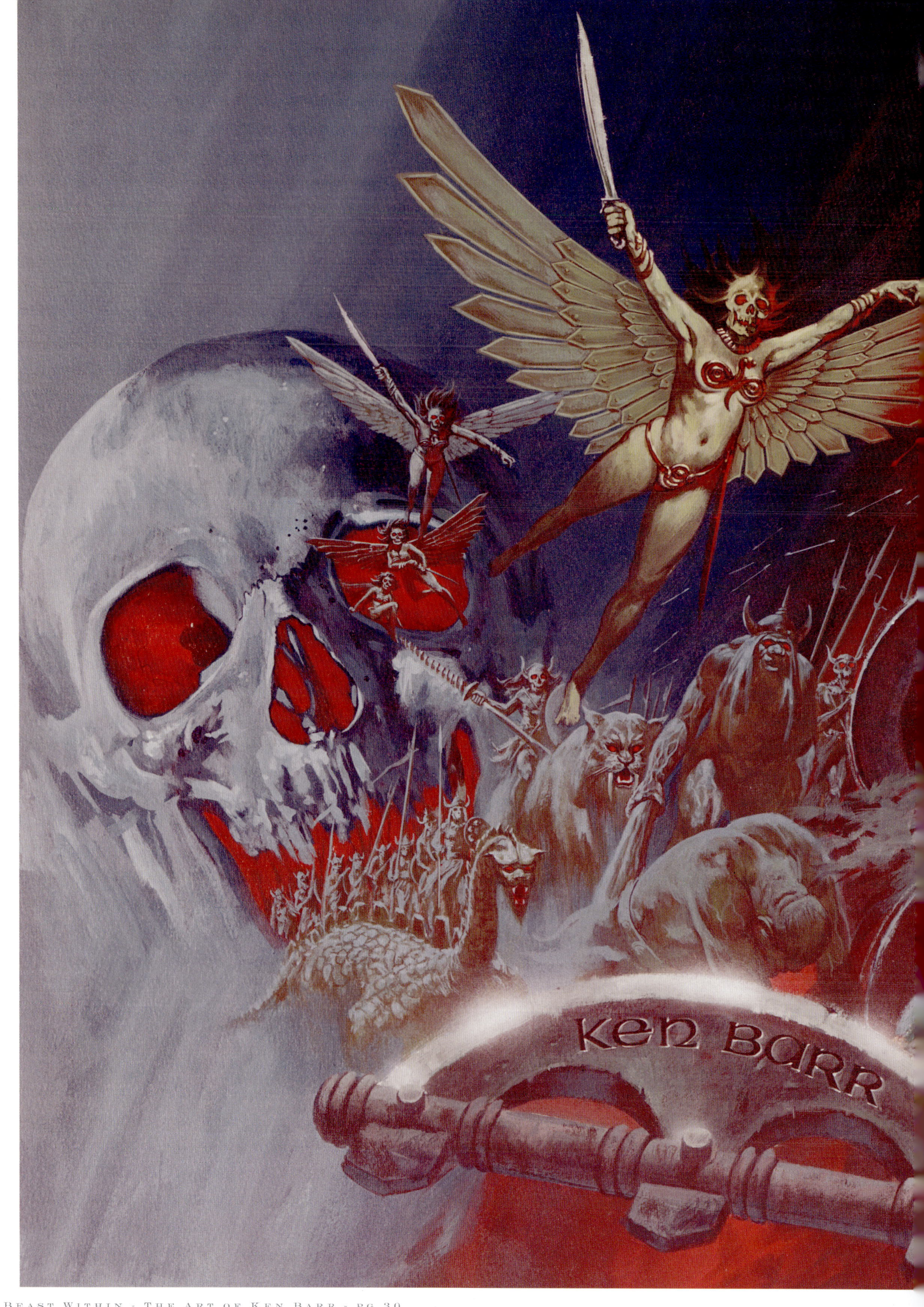
KEN BARR

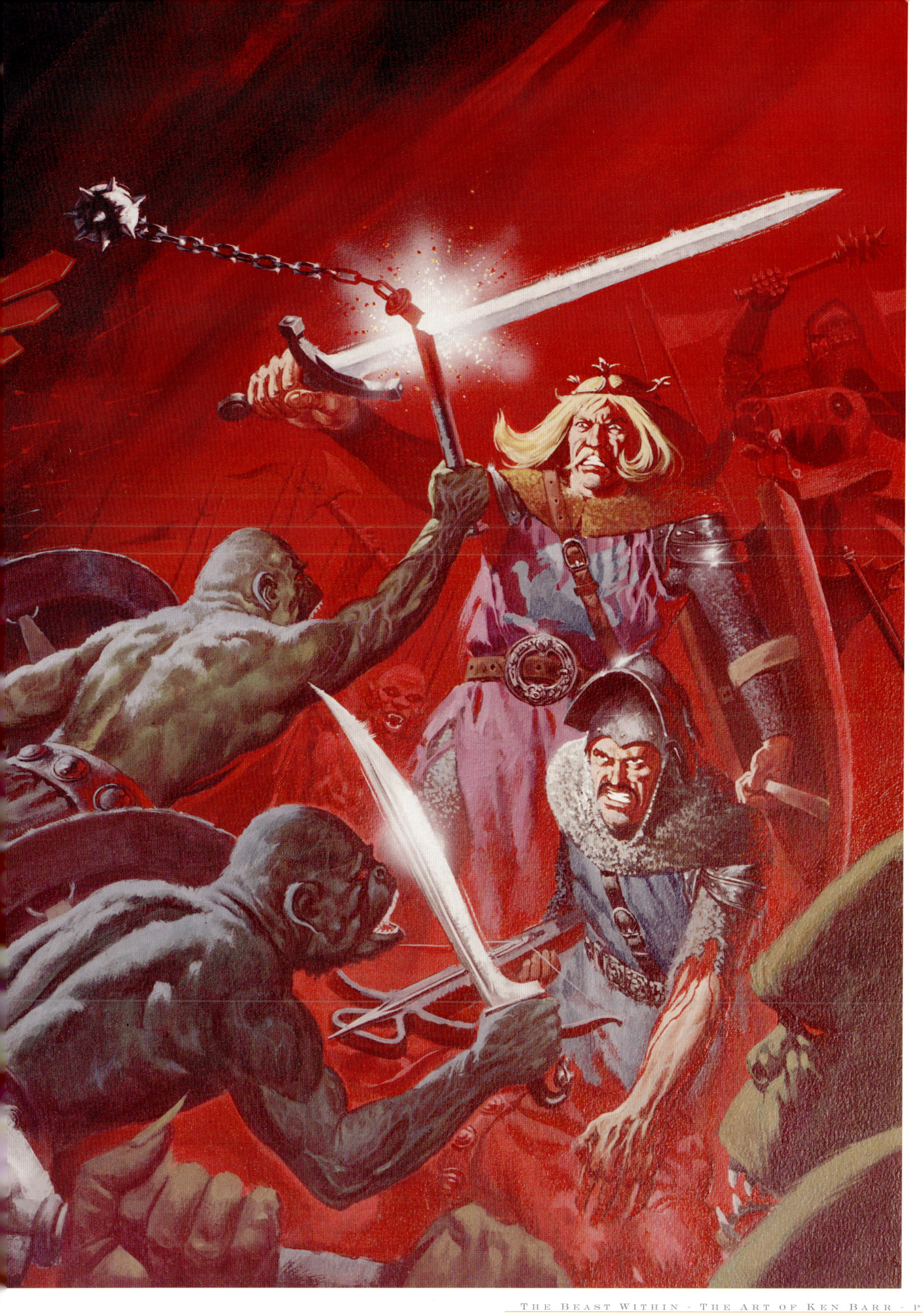

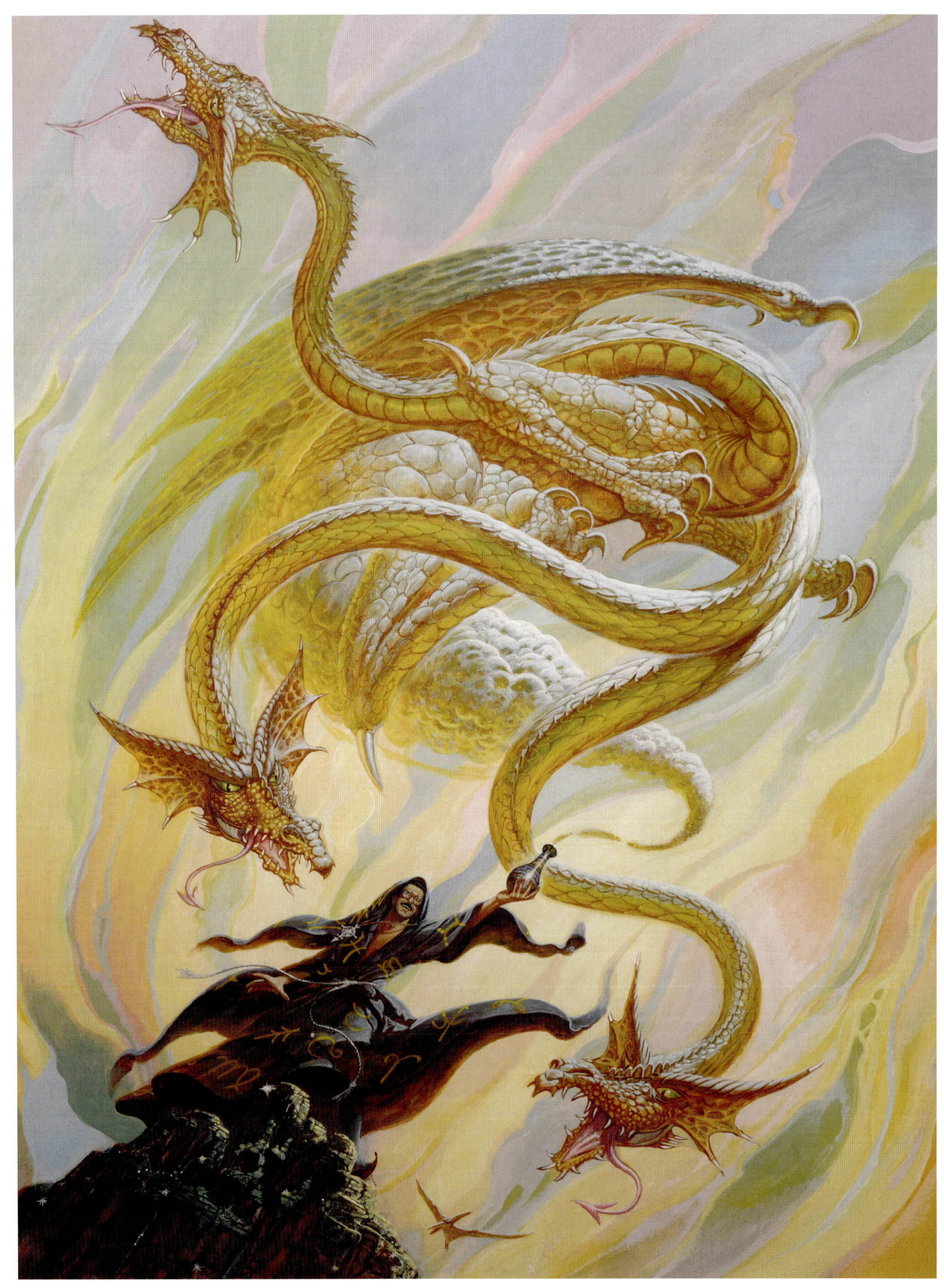

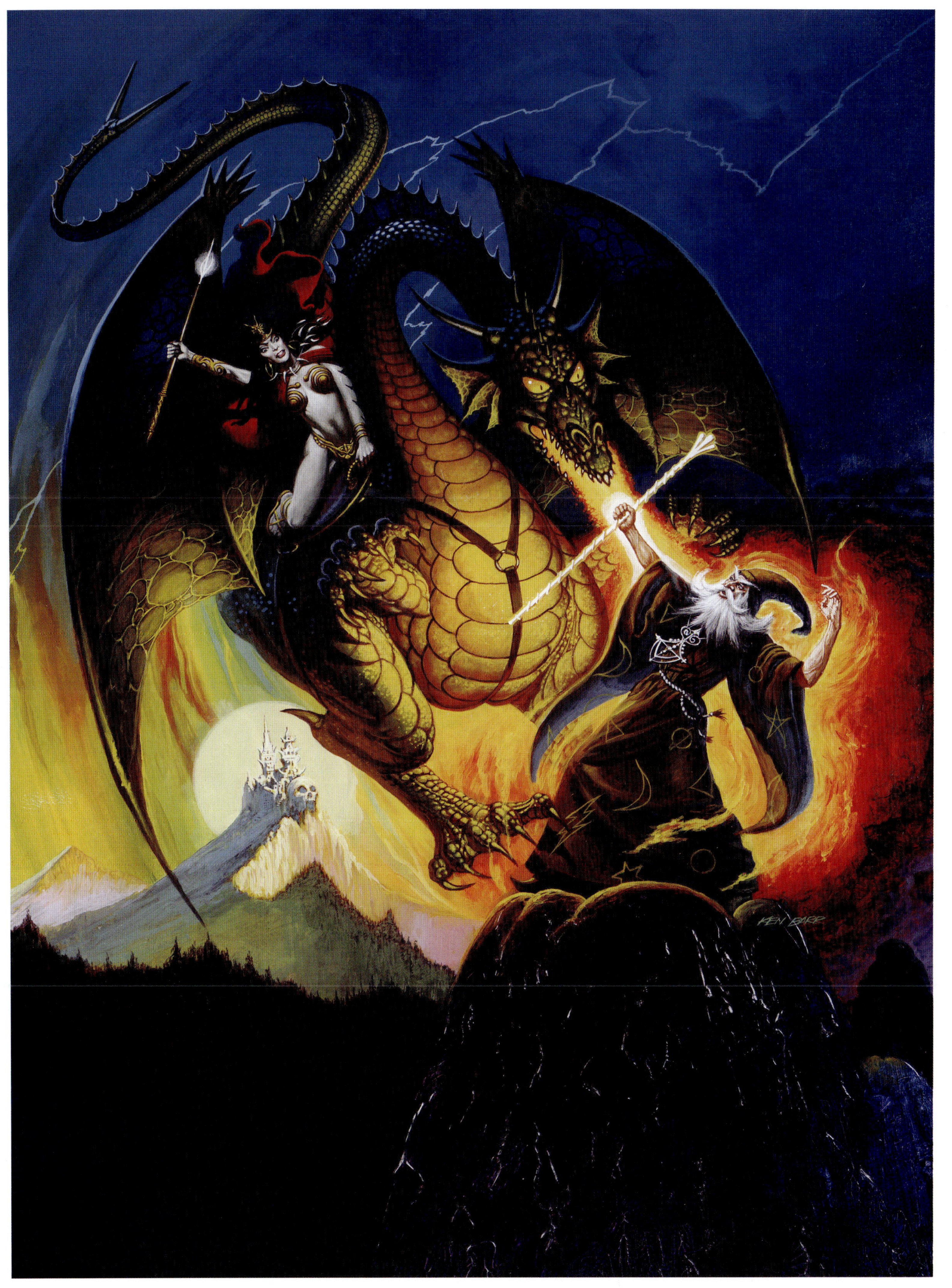
KEN BARR

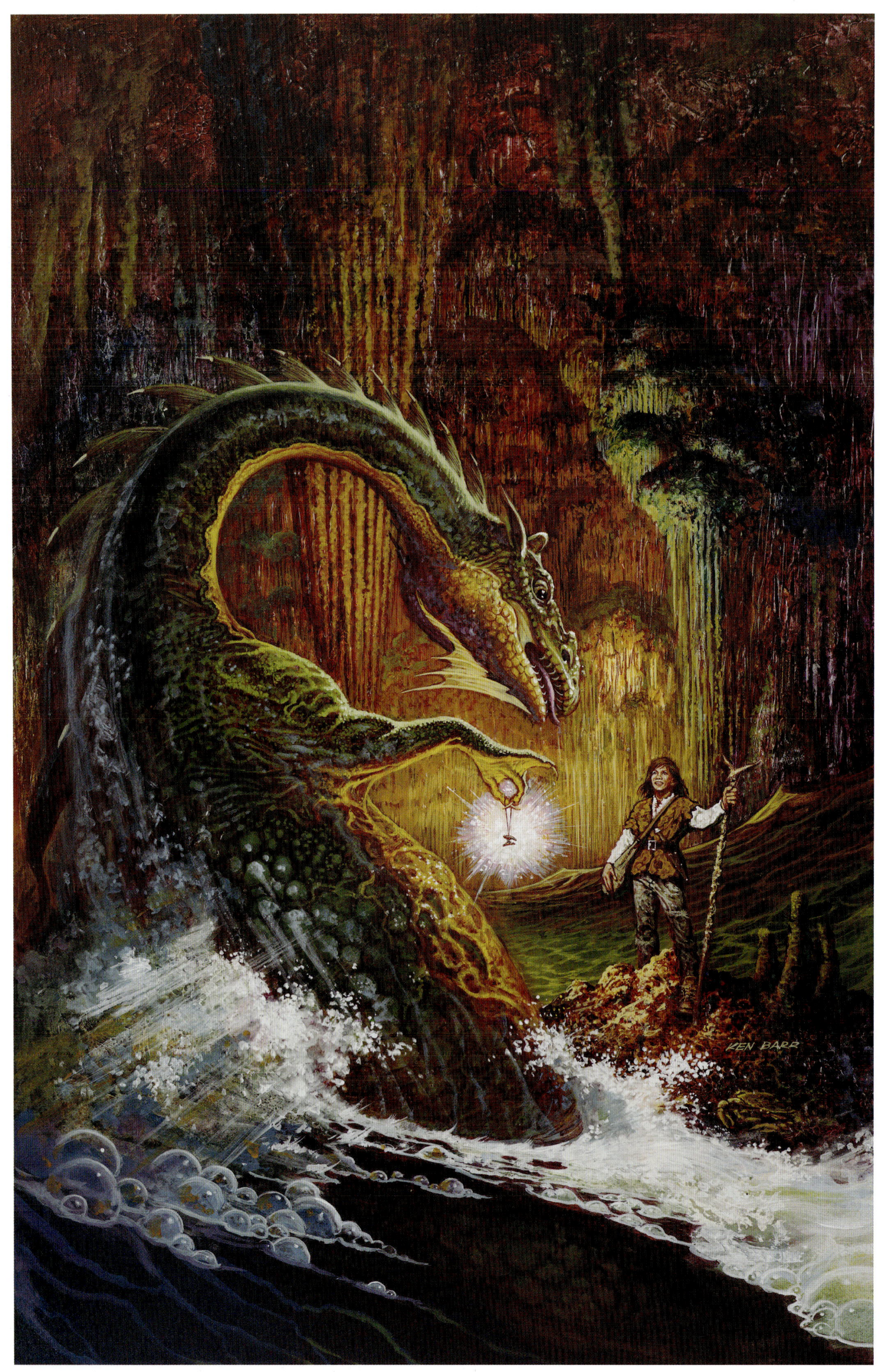
KEN BARR

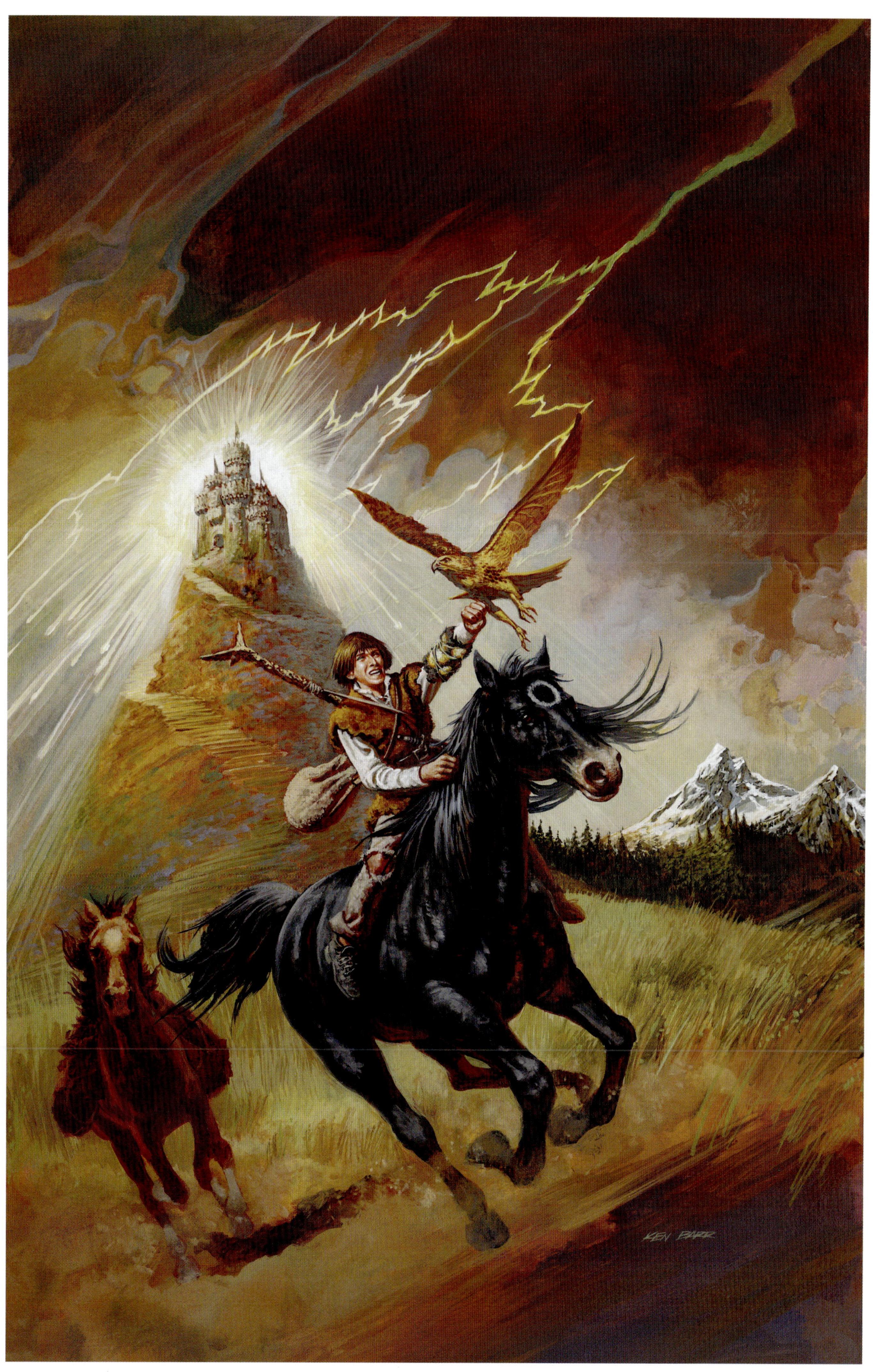
KEN BARR

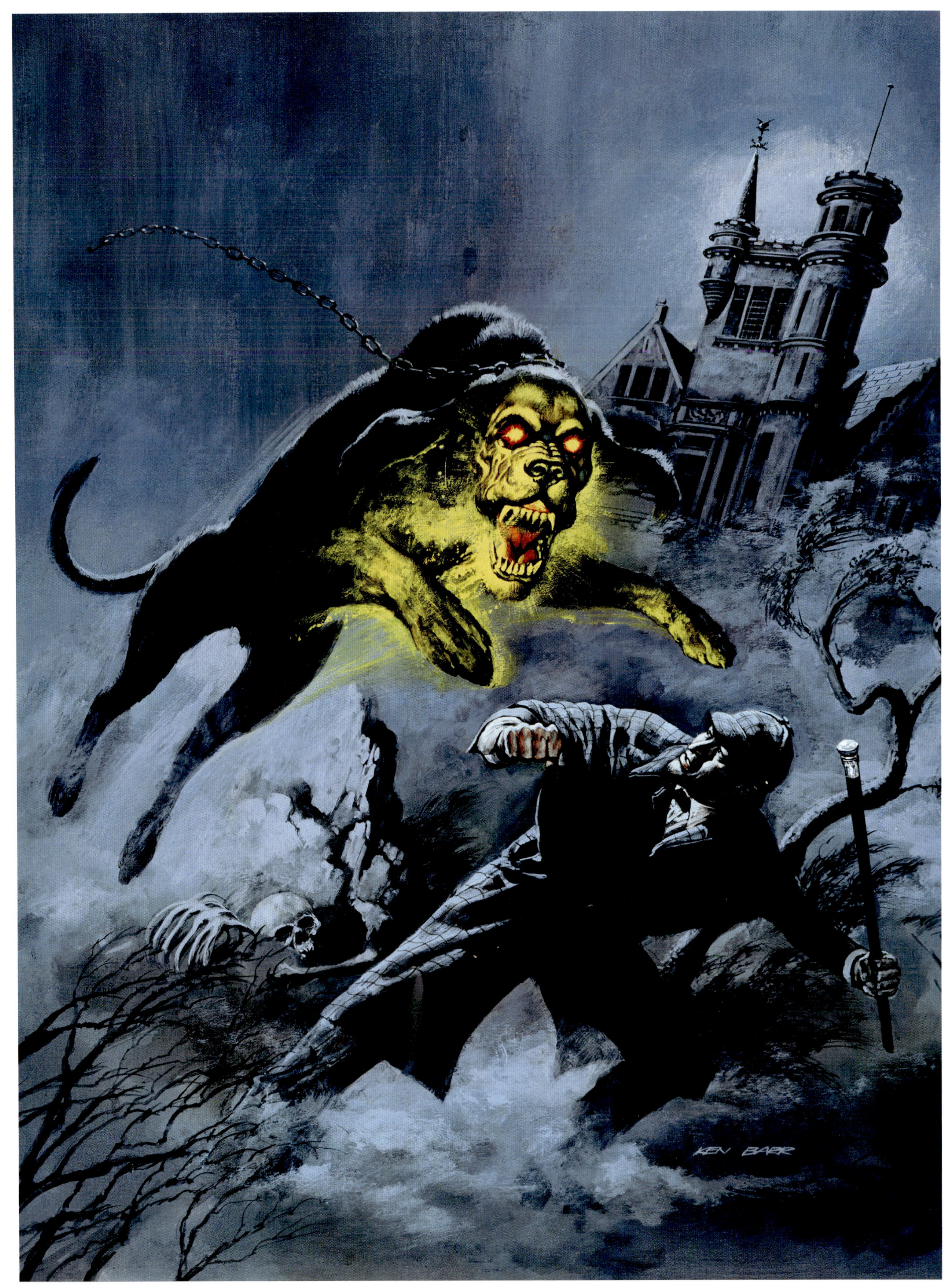
KEN BARR

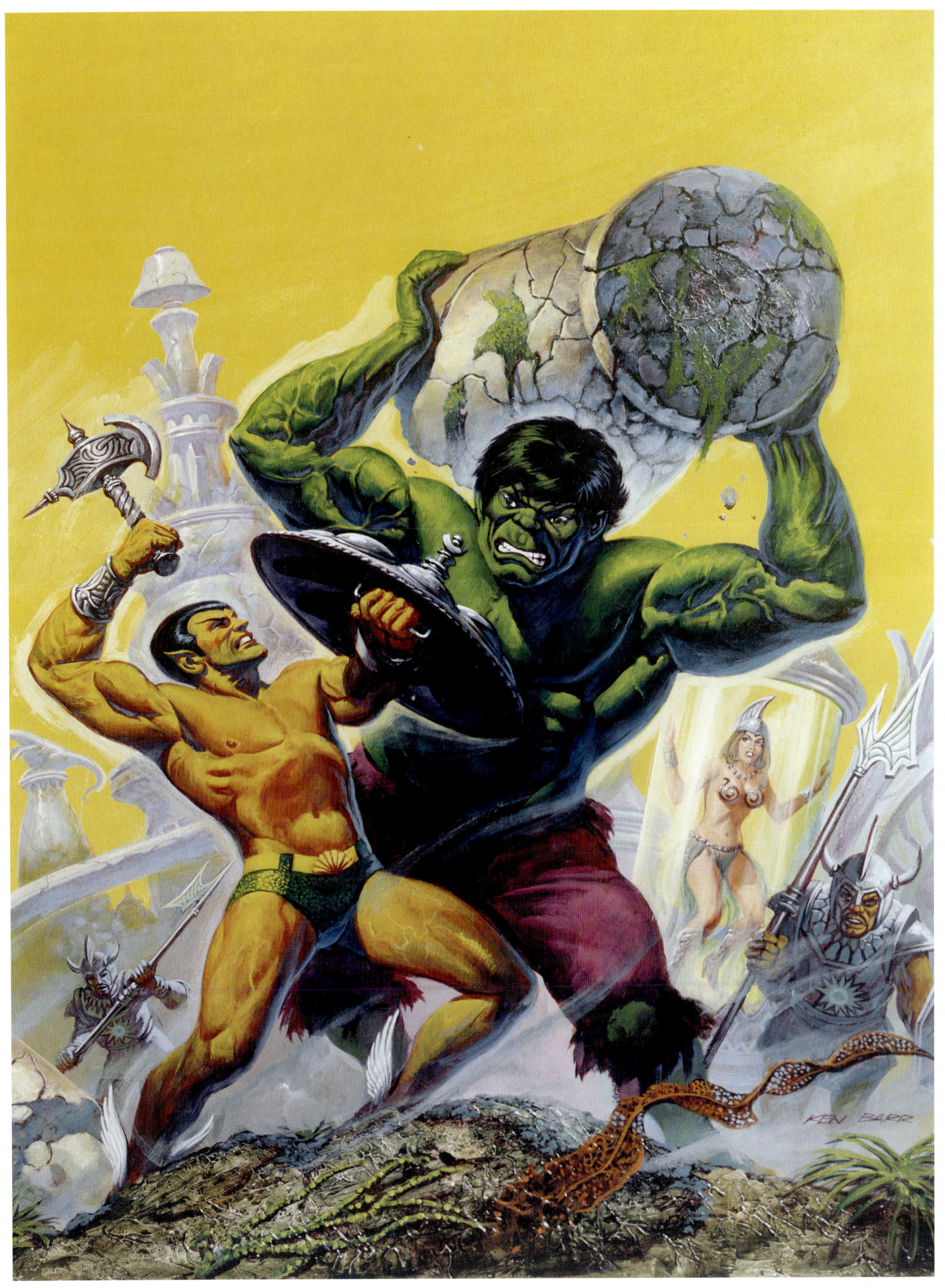
KEN BARR

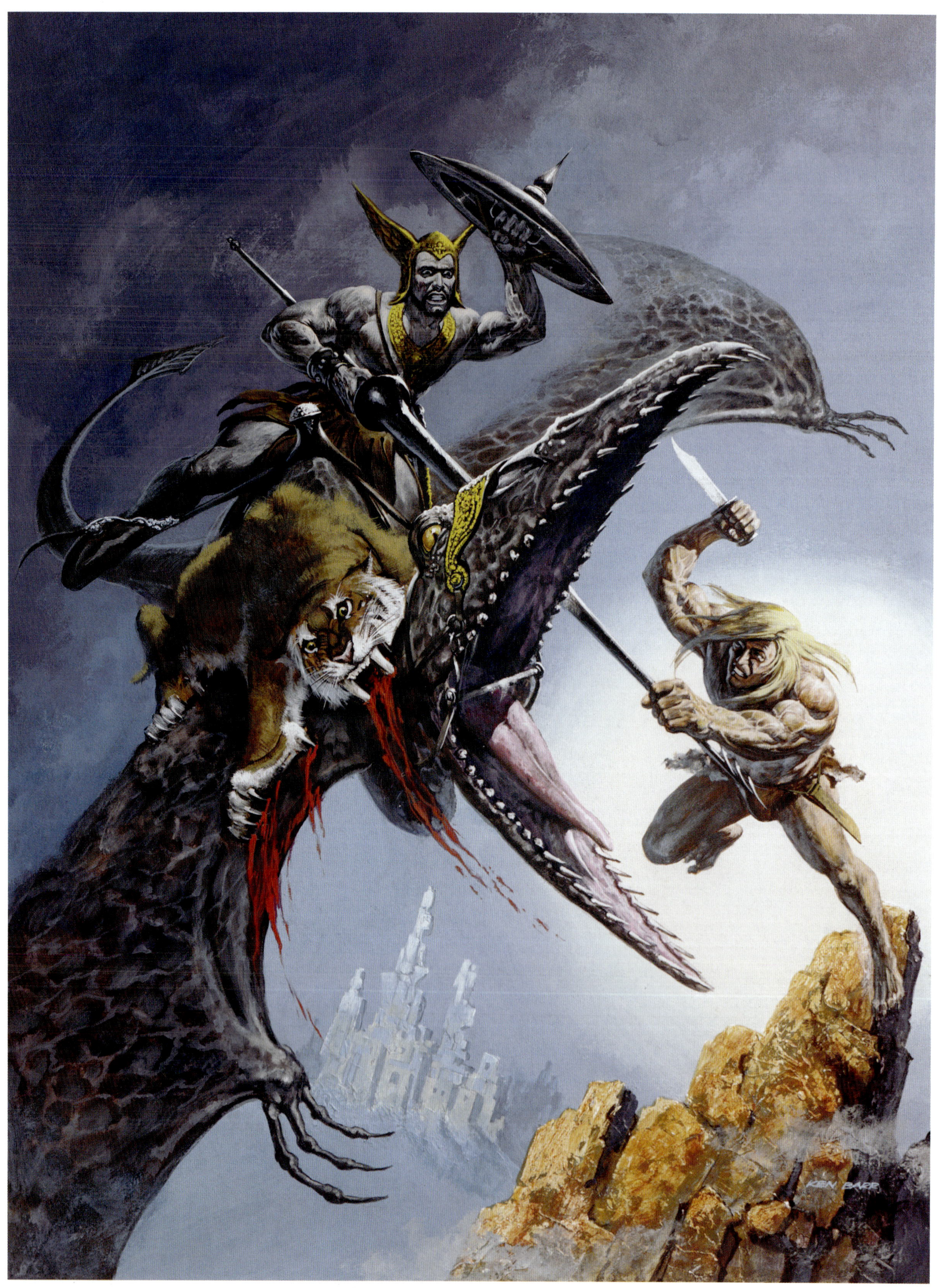
KEN BARR

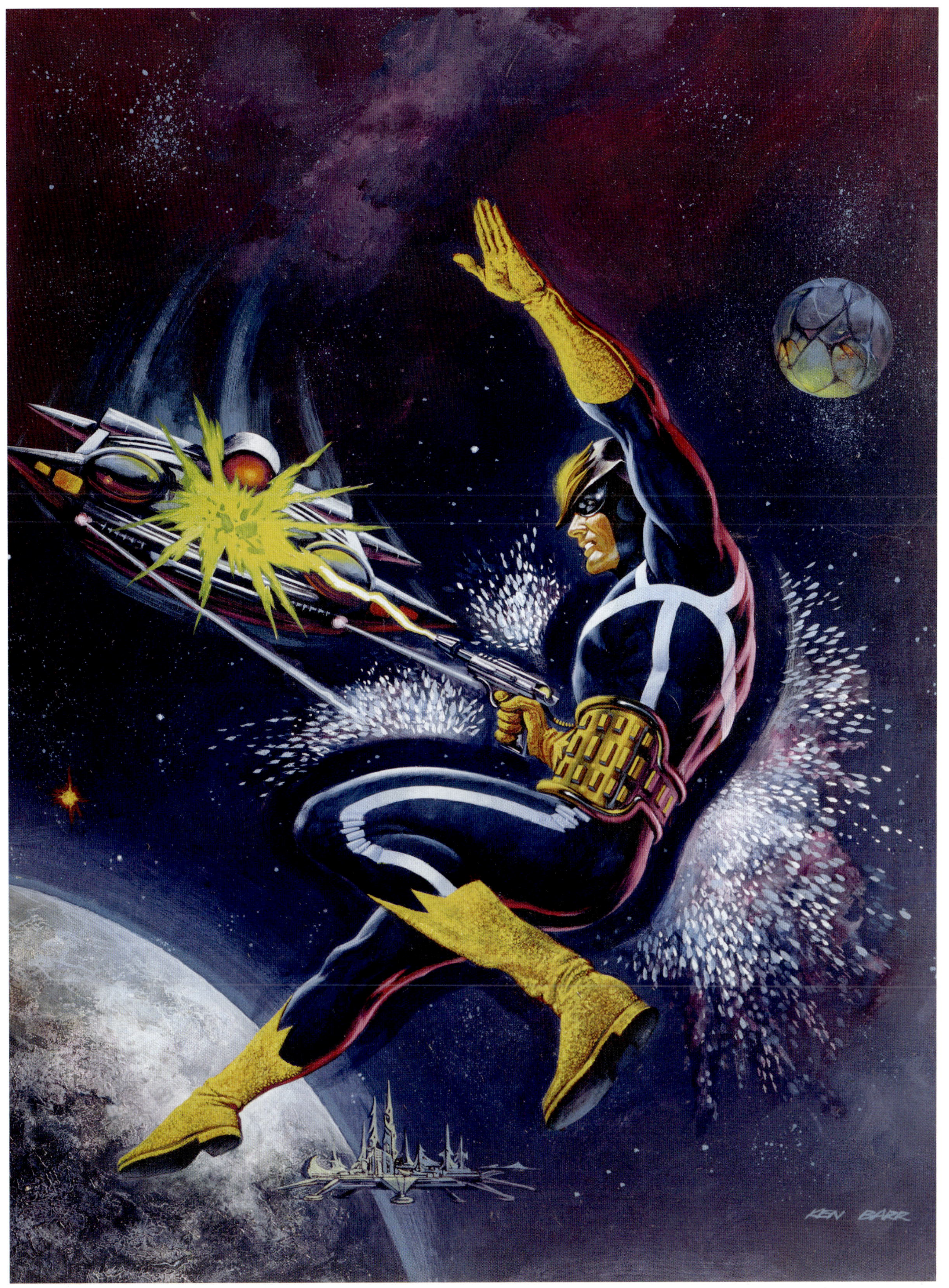
KEN BARR

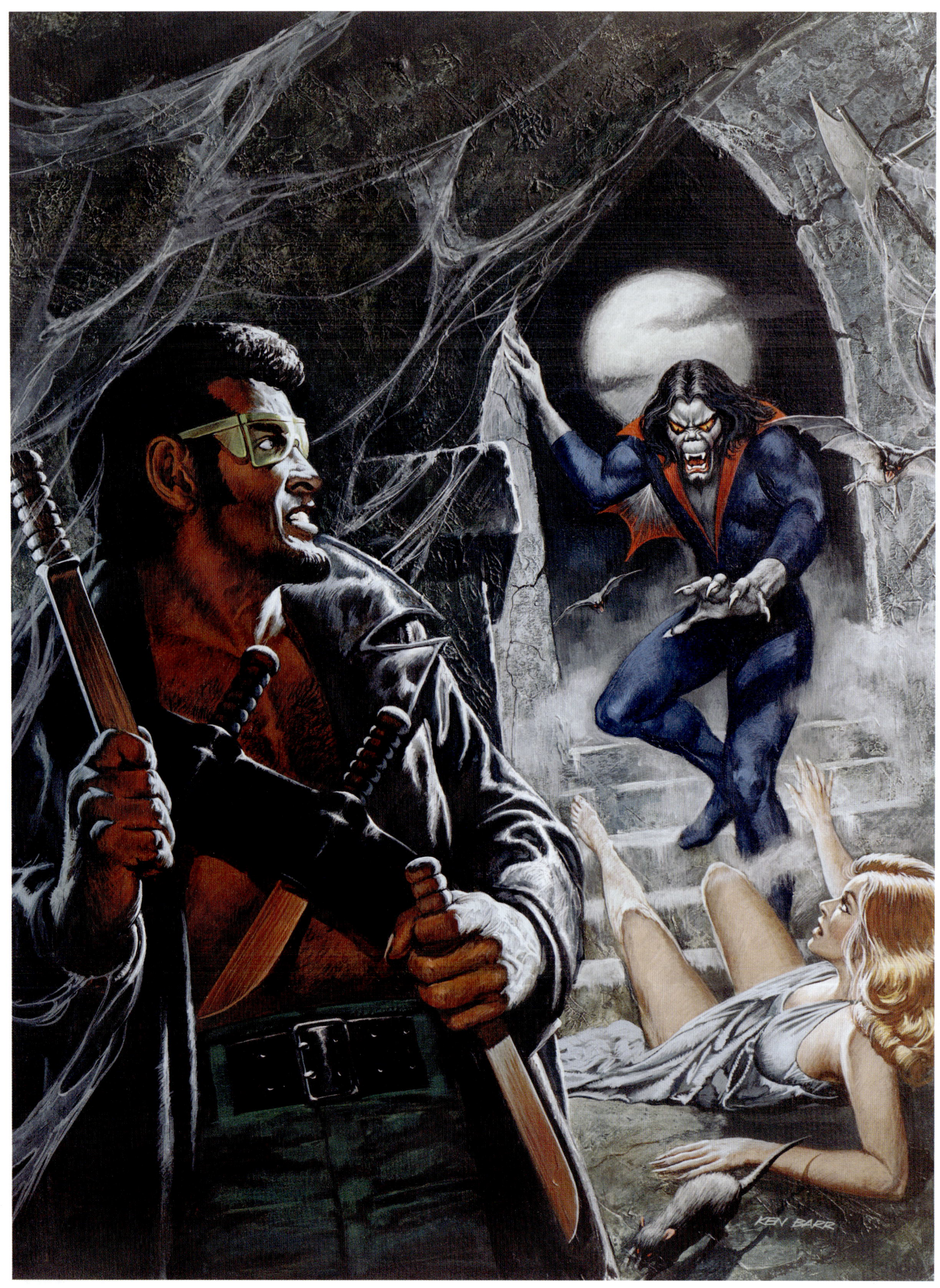
KEN BARR

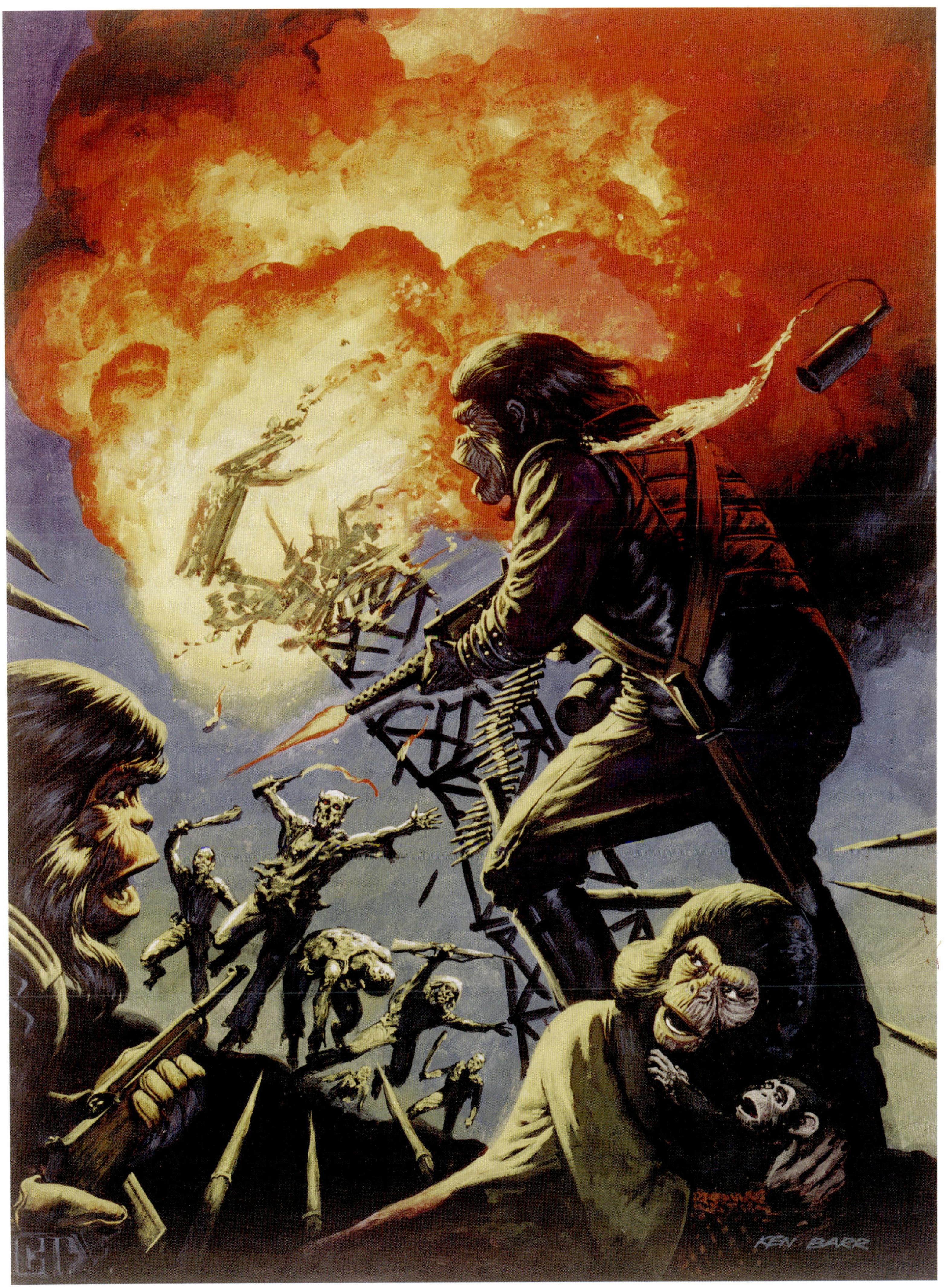
KEN BARR

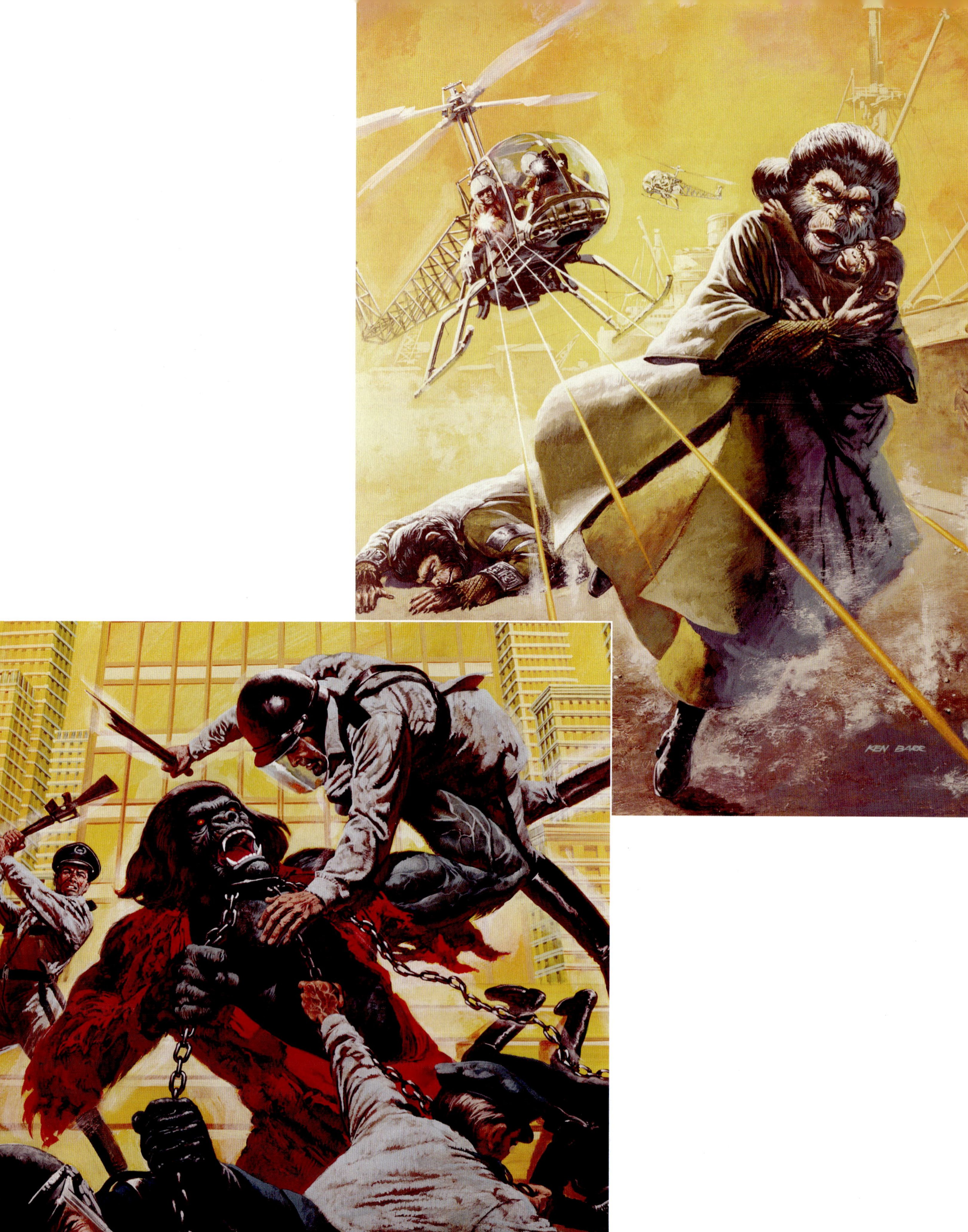
KEN BARR
KEN BARR

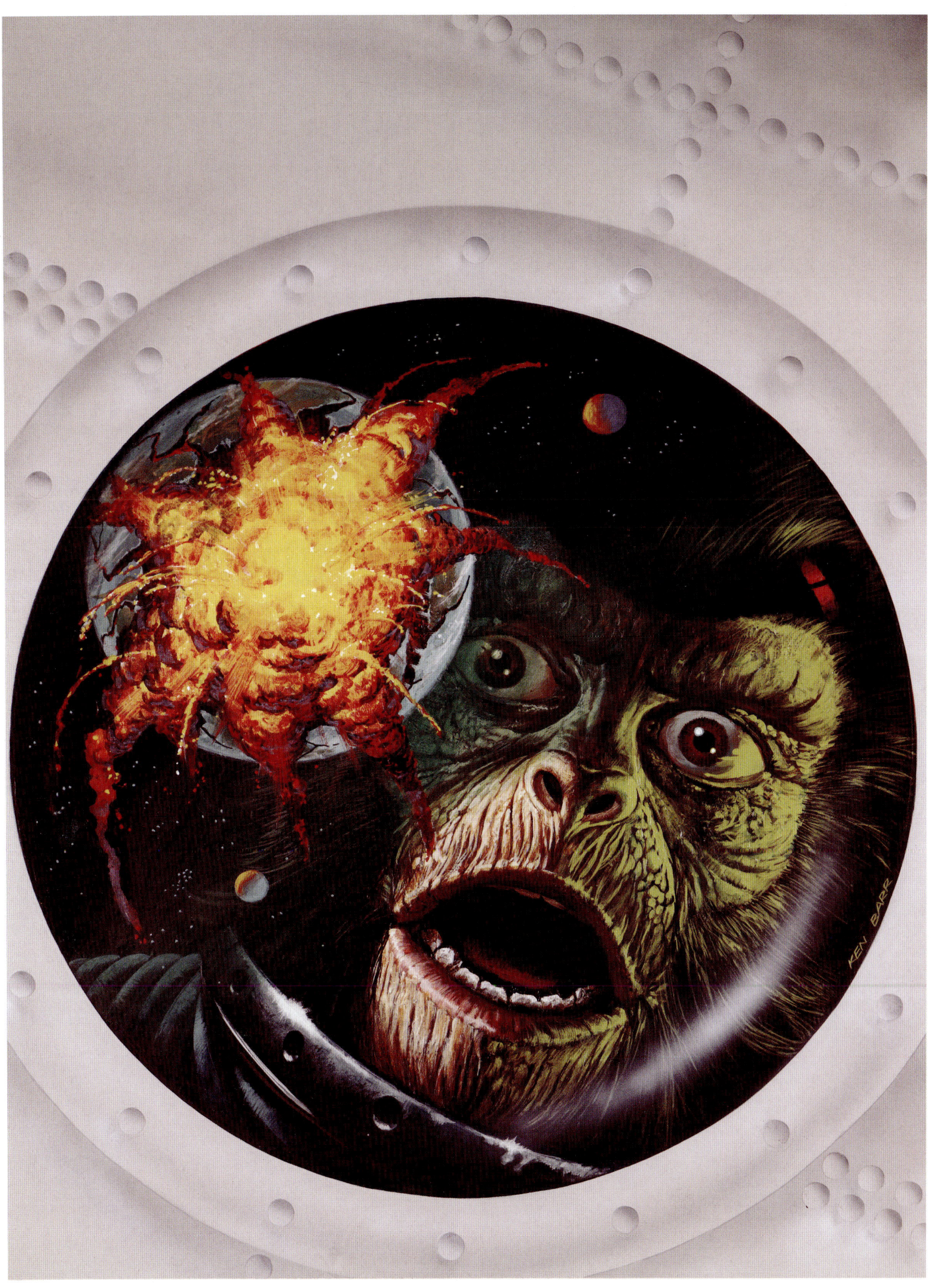
KEN BARR

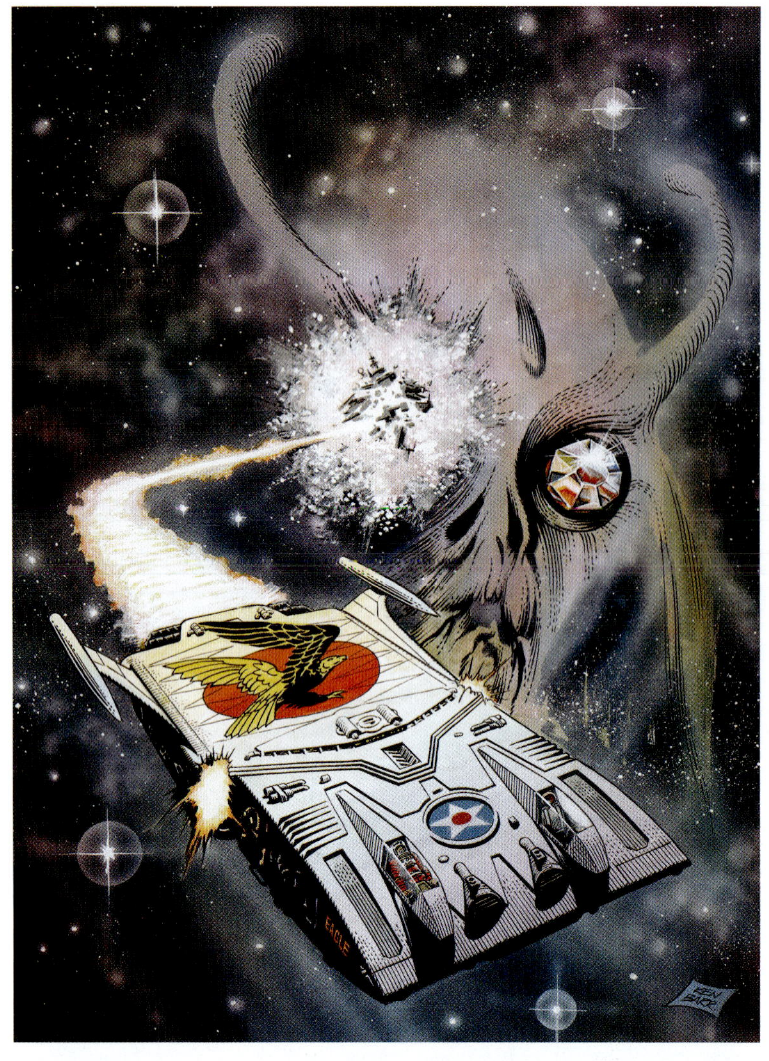
KEN BARR

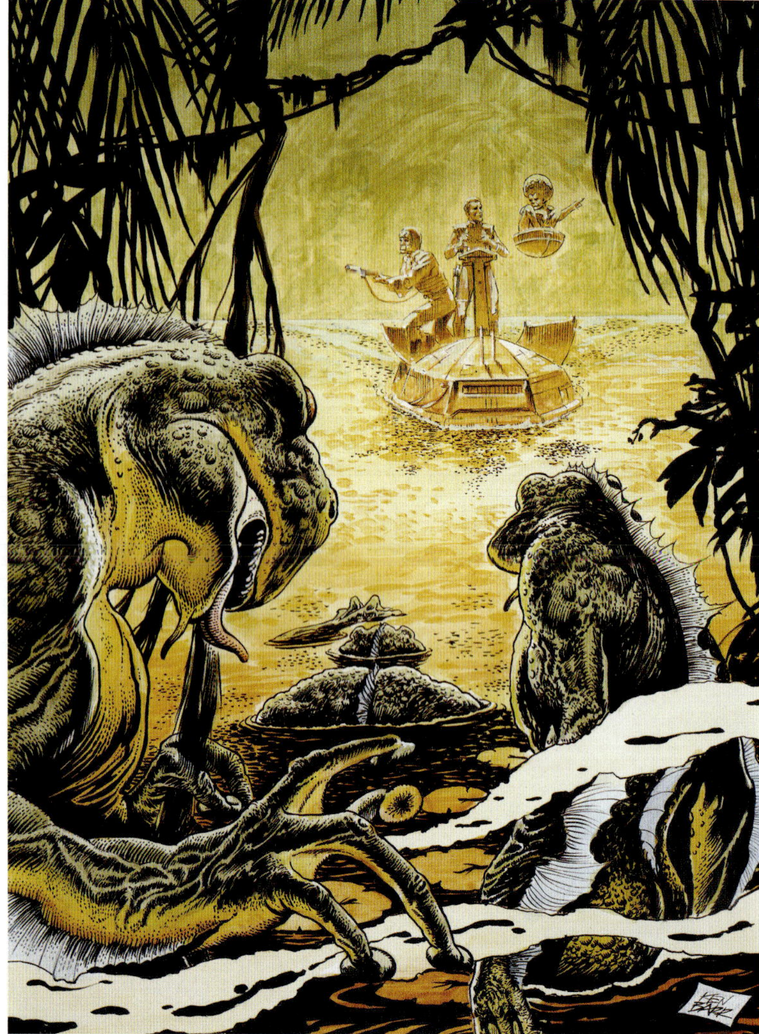
KEN BARR

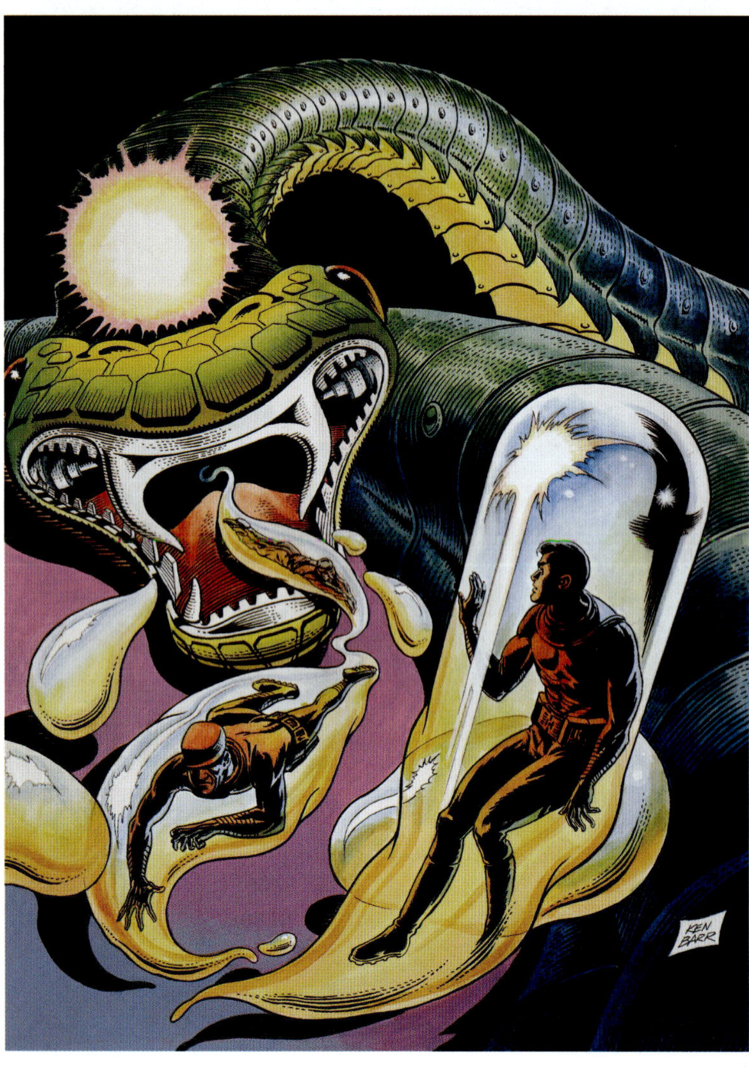
KEN BARR

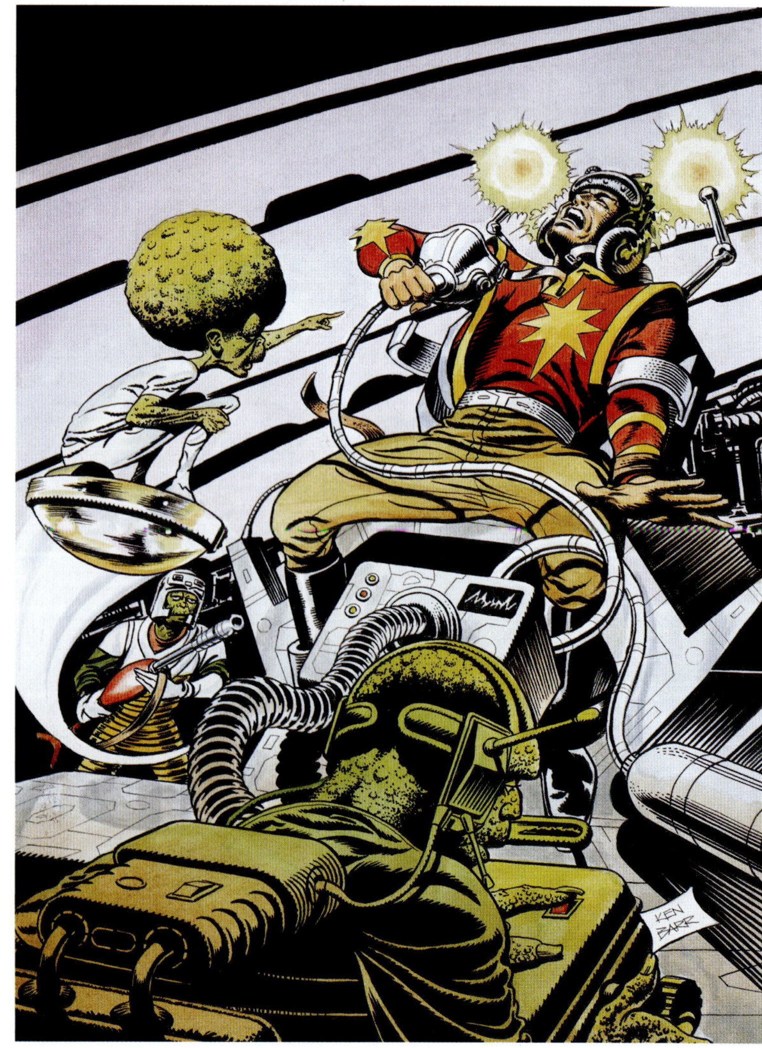
KEN BARR

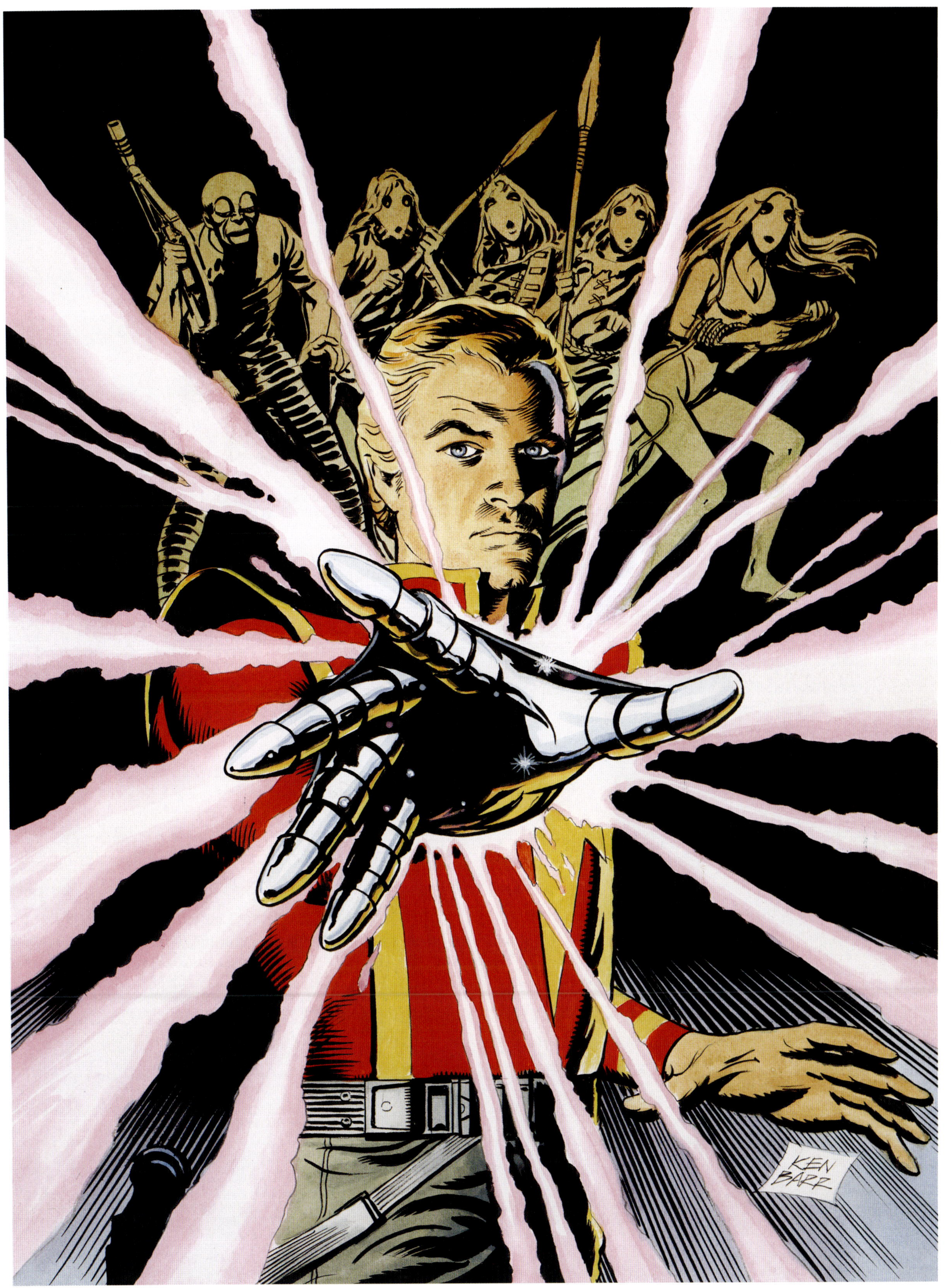
KEN BARR

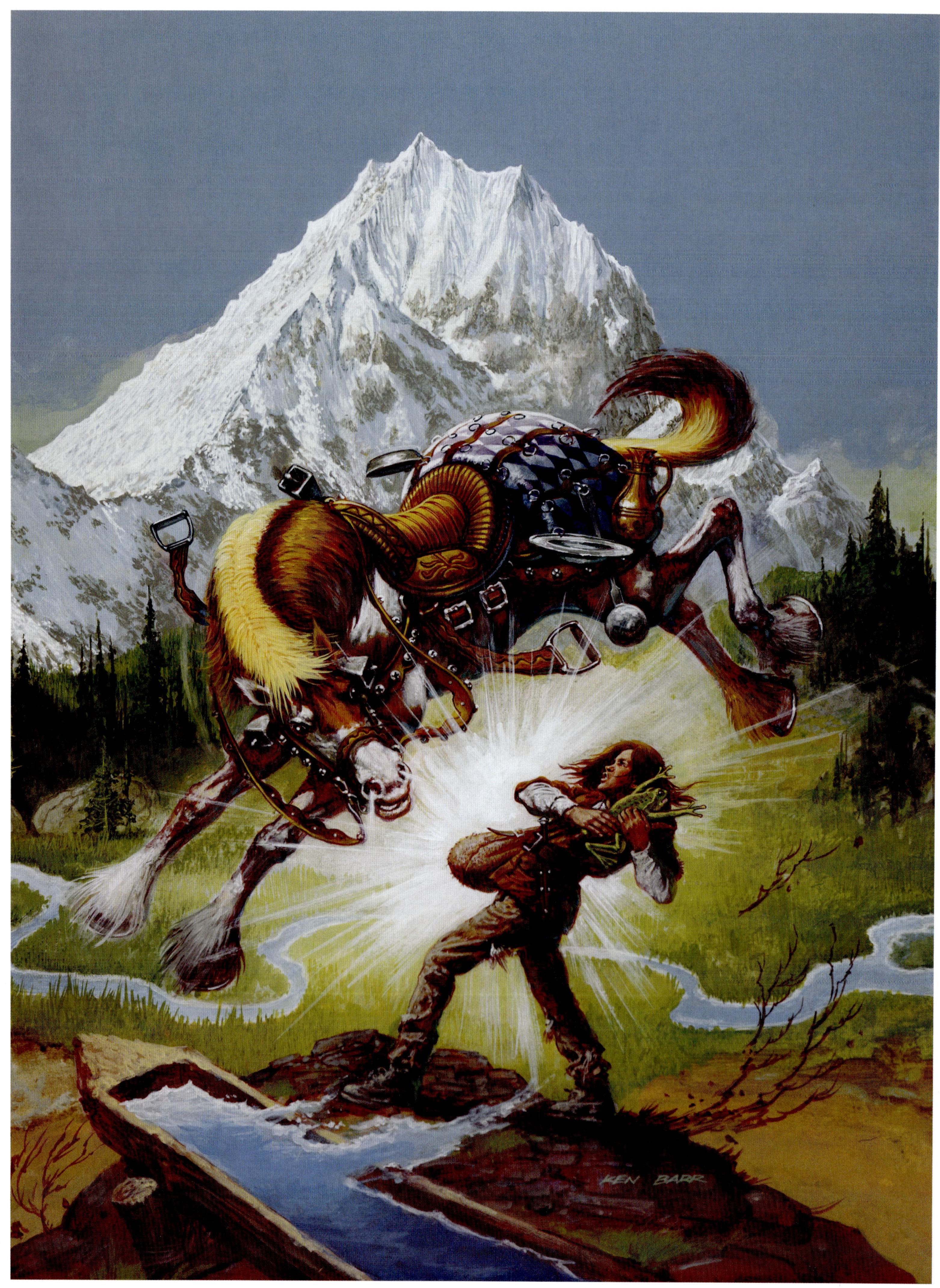
KEN BARR

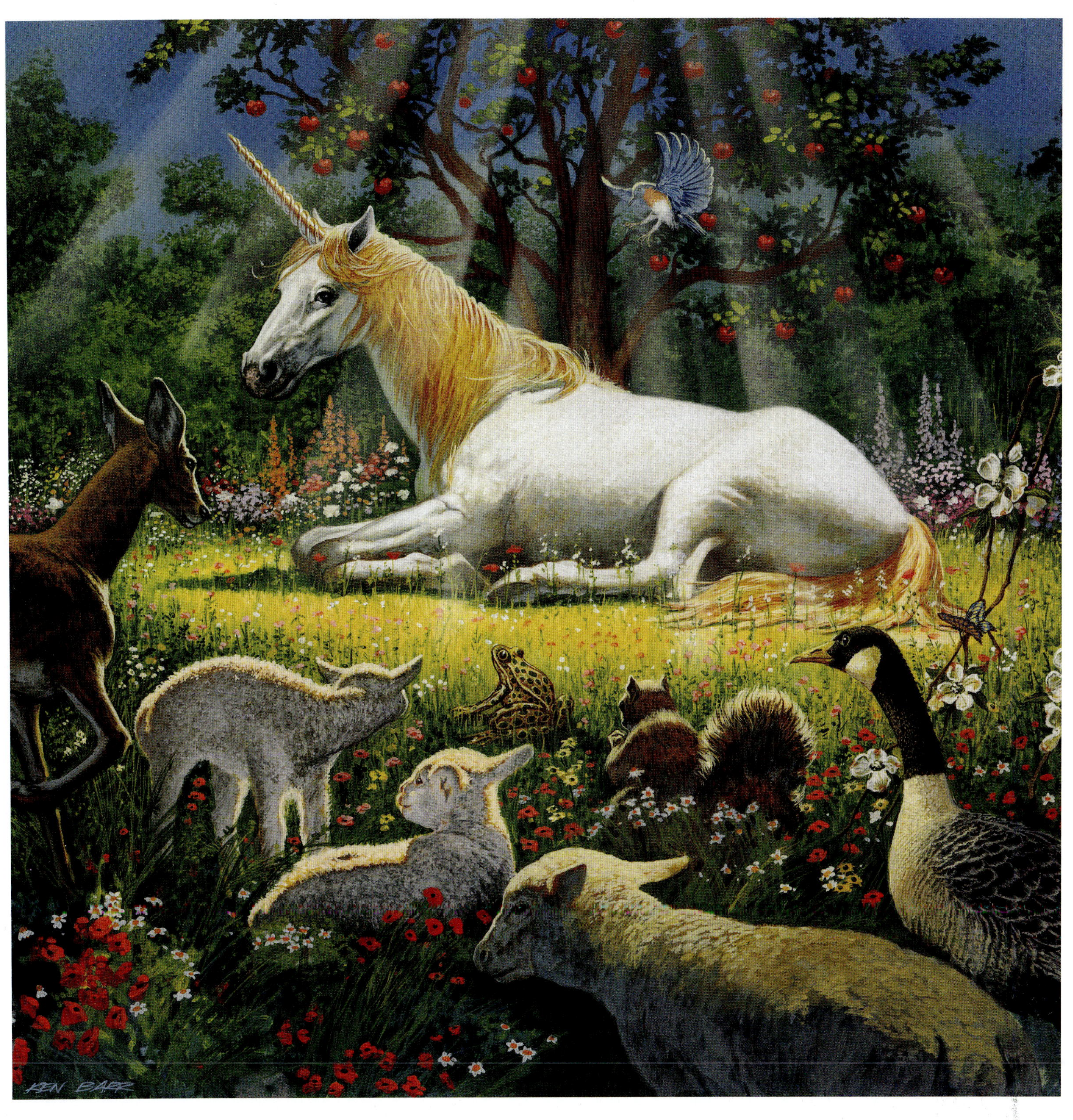
KEN BARR

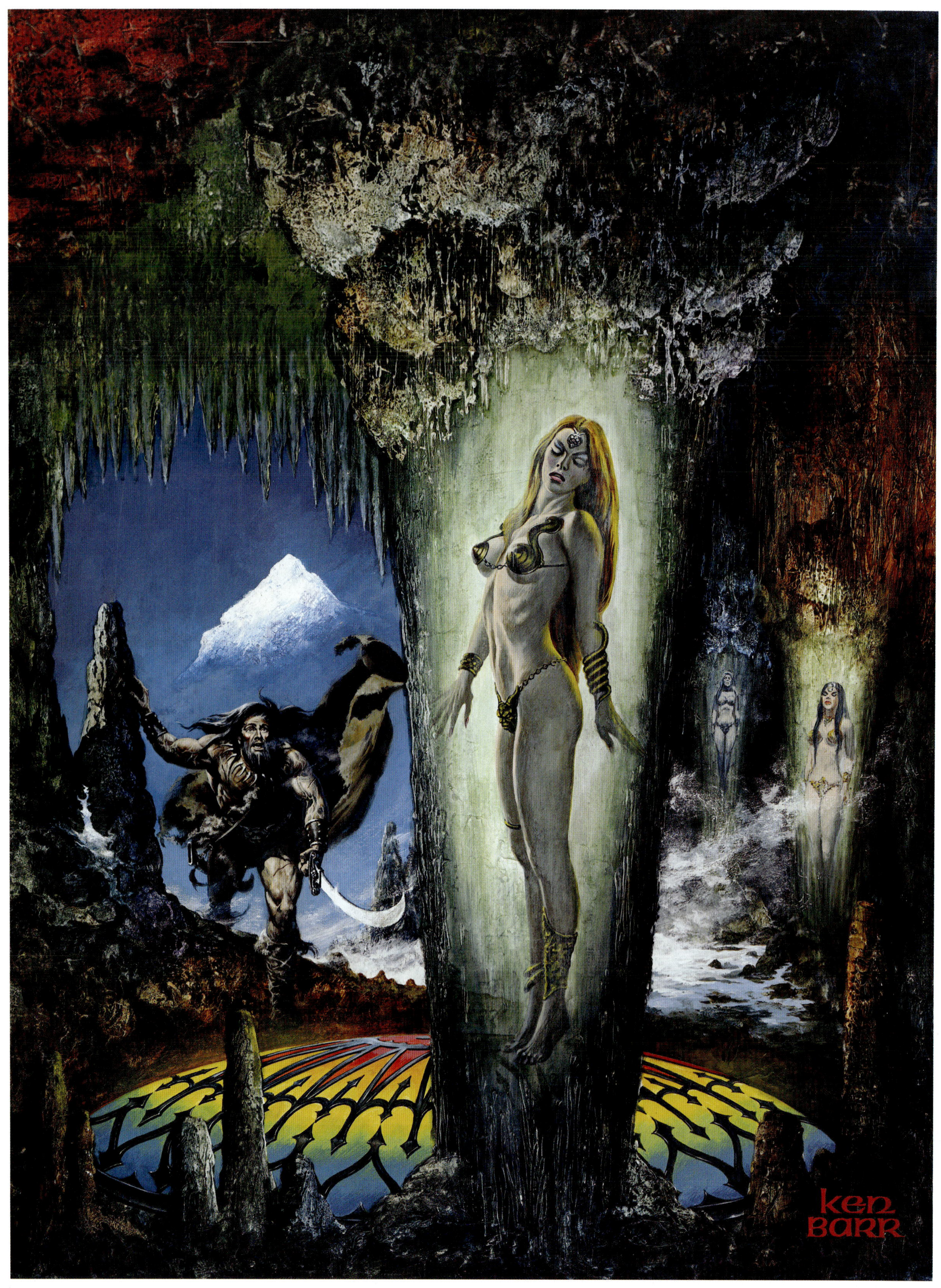
KEN
BARR